THE 50 GREATEST LETTERS FROM AMERICA'S WARS

THE 50 GREATEST LETTERS FROM AMERICA'S WARS

Edited by David H. Lowenherz

A BYRON PREISS BOOK

Crown Publishers
New York

Best efforts have been made to trace the ownership of letters under copyright and acknowledge their use. Grateful acknowledgement is made for permission to publish the following letters: Page 11: From *Dear America: Letters Home from Vietnam*, edited by Bernard Edelman for the New York Vietnam Veterans Memorial Commission, published by W. W. Norton & Company. Copyright © 1985 & 2002. Page 29: Reprinted by permission of Colonel (retired) David Hughes. Copyright © 2002 David Hughes. Page 48: Reprinted by permission of Steven Raab Autographs. Copyright © 2002 Steven Raab Autographs. Page 53: From *German Students' War Letters*, edited by Philipp Witkop. Page 69: From *Dear America: Letters Home from Vietnam*, edited by Bernard Edelman for the New York Vietnam Veterans Memorial Commission, published by W. W. Norton & Company. Copyright © 1985 & 2002. Page 79: Reprinted by permission of Great War Primary Document Archive, www.ukans.edu/~kansite/ww_one/medical/mmiss.htm. Page 91: From *Dear America: Letters Home from Vietnam*, edited by Bernard Edelman for the New York Vietnam Veterans Memorial Commission, published by W. W. Norton & Company. Copyright © 1985 & 2002. Page 121: From *German Students' War Letters*, edited by Philipp Witkop. Page 125: First published in *War Letters: Extraordinary Correspondence from American Wars* (Scribner, 2001), edited by Andrew Carroll. Copyright © Lorraine Lynch. Reprinted by permission of Lorraine Lynch and Andrew Carroll. Page 129: From *Letters from the Sand*. Courtesy US Postal Service and Kathleen Cronan Wyosnick. Page 133: From *Dear America: Letters Home from Vietnam*, edited by Bernard Edelman for the New York Vietnam Veterans Memorial Commission, published by W. W. Norton & Company. Copyright © 1985 & 2002. Page 139: Reprinted by permission of *European and Pacific Stars and Stripes*, a Department of Defense publication. © 2002 *European and Pacific Stars and Stripes*. Page 161: Reprinted by permission of former Chairman of the Joint Chiefs of Staff General Colin L. Powell. Page 177: Courtesy of Japanese American National Museum, a gift of Elizabeth Y. Yamada 93.75.31GP. Page 189: First published in *War Letters: Extraordinary Correspondence from American Wars* (Scribner, 2001), edited by Andrew Carroll. Copyright © Jo-ann Henningsen. Reprinted by permission of Jo-Ann Henningsen and Andrew Carroll. Page 192: First published in *War Letters: Extraordinary Correspondence from American Wars* (Scribner, 2001), edited by Andrew Carroll. Copyright © Alfred Puntasecca. Reprinted by permission of Alfred Puntasecca and Andrew Carroll. Page 201: Reprinted by permission of the Eisenhower Library. Page 215: Reprinted from *Madrid 1937: Letters of the Abraham Lincoln Brigade from the Spanish Civil War*. Copyright © 1996 Routledge. Page 219: Reprinted by permission of *European and Pacific Stars and Stripes*, a Department of Defense publication. © 2002 *European and Pacific Stars and Stripes*. Page 229: Reprinted from *The Mammoth Book of War Diaries & Letters*. Courtesy US Postal Service. Page 233: Courtesy Mako Sasaki and *The Concord Review*, www.tcr.org. Page 235: From *The Letters of PFC Richard E. Marks, USMC* by Richard E. Marks. Copyright © 1967 by Gloria D. Kramer, executrix of the Estate of Richard E. Marks. Reprinted by permission of HarperCollins Publishers Inc. Page 239: From *Dear America: Letters Home from Vietnam*, edited by Bernard Edelman for the New York Vietnam Veterans Memorial Commission, published by W. W. Norton & Company. Copyright © 1985 & 2002.

Photos copyright © 2002 HistoryPictures.com: 4, 13, 17, 25, 39, 47, 56, 66, 73, 80, 86, 97, 98, 117, 128, 135, 149, 152, 173, 200, 210, 214, 222, 228. Courtesy of Stephen S. Raab Autographs: 52. Courtesy of Lion Heart Autographs: 60. John Fitzgerald Kennedy Library: 94. Truman Presidential Library: 158. Gift of Elizabeth Y. Yamada of the Japanese American National Museum, 93.75.31: 178. Photo by Don LaVange: 184. Eisenhower Center, Kansas: 202. "L.B.F." Autograph note signed: Testament reporting death of Samuel Watson Vannuys, 10 October 1864 [postmark], (GLC 7687.154. The Gilder Lehrman Collection, courtesy of the Gilder Lehrman Institute of American History, New York): 228.

Published by Crown Publishers, New York, New York.
Member of the Crown Publishing Group, a division of Random House, Inc.
www.randomhouse.com

CROWN is a trademark and the Crown colophon
is a registered trademark of Random House, Inc.

Printed in the United States of America

Design by Mike Rivilis

Library of Congress Cataloging-in-Publication Data is available on request.

ISBN 0-8129-3275-7

10 9 8 7 6 5 4 3 2 1

First Edition

For my father-in-law, Leo Kaufman,
who slept on a bunk set atop a torpedo on the submarine USS
Irex from 1945 to 1946

—D. H. L.

A Note to the Reader

The letters reprinted in this collection are the most authentic and definitive versions available. To preserve the intimate and original nature of these letters we made a conscious decision to reproduce them as they were written, complete with spelling errors, grammatical imperfections, and, in some cases, antiquated terminology. We feel that these characteristics add to the charm and character of the letters. Besides, in the heat of impassioned expression, who has time for dictionaries?

CONTENTS

Famous Moments

Human Cost of War

Letters from Leaders

INTRODUCTION

While I read your letters, I'm not carrying guns and grenades. Instead I am going ice skating with David or walking through a department store to exchange a lamp shade. It is great to know your family's safe, living in a secure country; a country made secure by thousands upon thousands of men who have died for that country.

—Captain Rodney R. Chastant, Vietnam, October 19, 1967, killed in action one year later at the age of 25

You cannot qualify war in harsher terms than I will. War is cruelty, and you cannot refine it; and those who brought war into our country deserve all the curses and maledictions a people can pour out. I know I had no hand in making this war, and I know I will make more sacrifices to-day than any of you to secure peace.

—Union General William Tecumseh Sherman, September 12, 1864, to the Atlanta Mayor and City Council

I am a very fortunate person. My parents, who left Hitler's Germany prior to the outbreak of the Second World War, had the good sense and luck to immigrate to America where they met, prospered, and raised a family. They lived in a free society in a country consecrated with the blood of millions of men and women during its more than 225-year history.

I remember once asking my father where he was when he heard the news about Pearl Harbor on December 7, 1941. He recalled that it was a Sunday afternoon, and he was at home listening to the radio with my mother and their first child, a baby daughter. He could not recollect the details, but said he knew even then that this historic event would change his family's world forever. What were they *thinking?* I wondered, derisively, about the Japanese government when they made the decision to launch a surprise attack against the U.S. naval base at Pearl Harbor. Obviously, they had planned their raid with care, fully intending to seriously damage our defenses and bring the war to U.S. soil. But did they really consider the consequences of their act?

Then I turned the question over in my mind again: What were *they* thinking? meaning the American sailors and officers on board their ships as they ran to their battle stations that morning. Did they even have the opportunity to think, or were they just reacting in a desperate attempt to protect their ships and themselves? By then, my thoughts had raced ahead four years to the crew of the *Enola Gay* when they dropped the first atomic bomb over Hiroshima. What were they thinking, and what was President Harry Truman thinking when he decided to drop the bomb? Did the thousands who were incinerated in Hiroshima and later in Nagasaki even have time to think?

This book addresses the question, what were the nurses, loved ones, prisoners of war, pilots, generals, infantrymen, and officers thinking? The answer is, of course, they were thinking about survival, duty to country, and returning home. But many also thought about the prejudice they faced due to race or religion, vengeance, the death of a comrade, or the fate of civilians caught in the cross-fire—and some even reflected on their enemy's defeat.

But this is not a collection of blood-and-guts letters from the trenches. I have read enough of those in my nearly quarter of a century as a dealer in rare letters and manuscripts. Such letters, while astonishing in the dramatic retelling of events on the battlefield, are fundamentally not very compelling when read in quantity. *The 50 Greatest Letters from America's Wars* explores some of the more unusual, even fascinating aspects of men and women at war. It poses questions of its own: How did General Sherman justify the evacuation of the entire city of Atlanta? What did a fourteen-year-old boy write to his parents the day before he was killed in action during the Civil War? What did a nurse close to the front lines during World War I write as she valiantly tried to save the lives and nurture the spirits of the wounded? How did George Washington feel about his poorly clothed and ill-fed troops at Valley Forge? What did Theodore Roosevelt truly think about war just days after his famous charge up San Juan Hill? The answers surprised me, and I think they will surprise you, too.

There are also some remarkably candid and unique letters in this collection, including one written by a GI describing his looting in Germany after WWII, and a life-saving letter scratched on a coconut shell by a Navy lieutenant whose future career would change the course of history. There are a few documents from the "other" side, including a heartfelt letter by a German soldier from the trenches during Christmas 1914, and a note by a kamikaze pilot before taking off on his final mission.

Some letters are unusual because they were penned just hours before the writer died. What was the GI in Korea thinking when he sent his final words to his girlfriend in response to her Dear John letter? What did the Civil War commandant of the notorious Andersonville prison think were his chances of clemency when he wrote President Andrew Johnson pleading for mercy the night before his execution?

I recently spoke with a WWII vet, the only Jewish officer in his battalion, who reminisced about prejudice among his troops. He was surprised to learn about a Jewish officer's letter resigning his commission during the Civil War in response to General Grant's anti-Semitic General Order No. 11. That letter is included in this book, too.

He also told me that although the combat experience was horrible, it was relatively infrequent—much of the time was spent tending to the necessary chores that soldiers, sailors, and airmen have, but included opportunities for letter writing, as well. I suspect that some even had a moment to speculate why commanders were about to order them, perhaps unprepared, into harm's way. What are *they thinking?* they must have wondered.

What makes these letters great? While the content is fascinating, to paraphrase Dr. Samuel Johnson, nothing so clears the mind as the sight of the gallows. Many of these letters are superb examples of the writers' ability to express powerful emotions while in the throes of extraordinary circumstances. Dorothy Parker once asked Ernest Hemingway what he meant by "guts," and he replied, "Grace under pressure." Each letter in this collection has that quality—they are gutsy, even heroic, and yet filled with grace. I hope you agree.

Why Are We Here?

PRESIDENT ABRAHAM LINCOLN TO JAMES C. CONKLING,

Washington, D.C., August 26, 1863,

Civil War

Considered by many to be one of America's greatest presidents, Abraham Lincoln presided over this country's severest test, the Civil War. Though his visage has become an American icon, it is his words that have been sewn into the moral fabric of our country. Among the presidents, he may be the greatest writer. His letters and speeches are a unique mix of logic and vision, plainly expressed through the imaginative power of emotional and moral certitude. Lincoln's overriding goal during his presidency was to reunite the United States by any means possible. Nearly one year before writing Conkling, Lincoln contacted newspaper journalist Horace Greeley, writing, "I would save the Union. I would save it the shortest way under the Constitution. The sooner the national authority can be restored, the nearer the Union will be the 'Union as it was.' If there be those who would not save the Union unless they could at the same time save slavery, I do not agree with them. If there be those who would not save the Union unless they could at the same time destroy slavery, I do not agree with them. My paramount object in this struggle is to save the Union, and is not either to save or to destroy slavery. If I could save the Union without freeing any slave, I would do it and if I could save it by freeing all the slaves, I would do it; and if I could save it by freeing some and leaving others alone, I would also do that. What I do about slavery, and the colored race, I do because I believe it helps to save the Union; and what I forbear, I forbear because I do not believe it would help to save the Union."

In the thick of the Civil War, Lincoln turned to his longtime friend James C. Conkling for a small favor. Born in New York City in 1816, Conkling moved to Springfield, Illinois, in 1838, where he established a law practice. A well-known orator who was elected mayor in 1845, he helped form the Illinois Republican Party in 1856. The president, unable to leave Washington, asked Conkling to read the following letter to Union supporters scheduled for a rally in Springfield on September 3, 1863, explaining, "I cannot leave here now. Herewith is a letter instead. You are one of the best public readers. I have but one suggestion. Read it very slowly. And now God bless you and all good Union-men."

My Dear Sir,

Your letter inviting me to attend a mass-meeting of unconditional Union-men, to be held at the Capitol of Illinois, on the 3d day of September, has been received.

It would be very agreeable to me, to thus meet my old friends, at my own home; but I can not, just now, be absent from here, so long as a visit there, would require.

The meeting is to be of all those who maintain unconditional devotion to the Union; and I am sure my old political friends will thank me for tendering, as I do, the nation's gratitude to those other noble men, whom no partizan malice, or partizan hope, can make false to the nation's life.

There are those who are dissatisfied with me. To such I would say: You desire peace; and you blame me that we do not have it. But how can we attain it? There are but three conceivable ways. First, to suppress the rebellion by force of arms. This I am trying to do. Are you for it? If you are, so far we are agreed. If you are not for it, a second way is to give up the Union. I am against this. Are you for it? If you are, you should say so plainly. If you are not for force, nor yet for dissolution, there only remains some imaginable compromise. I do not believe any compromise, embracing the maintenance of the Union, is now possible. All I learn, leads to a directly opposite belief. The strength of the rebellion, is its military—its army. That army dominates all the country, and all the people, within its range. Any offer of terms made by any man or men within that range, in opposition to that army, is simply nothing for the present; because such man or men, have no power whatever to enforce their side of a compromise, if one were made with them. To illustrate. Suppose refugees from the South, and peace men of the North, get together in convention, and frame and proclaim a compromise embracing a restoration of the Union; in what way can that compromise be used to keep Lee's army out of Pennsylvania? Meade's army can keep Lee's army out of Pennsylvania; and I think, can ultimately drive it out of existence. But no paper compromise, to which the controllers of Lee's army are not agreed, can at all affect that army. In an effort at such compromise we should waste time, which the enemy would improve to our disadvantage; and that would be all. A compromise, to be effective, must be made either with those who control the rebel army, or with the people first liberated from the domination of that army, by the success of our own army. Now allow me to assure you, that no word or intimation, from that rebel army, or from any of the men controlling it, in relation to any peace compromise, has ever come to my knowledge or belief. All charges and insinuations to the contrary, are deceptive and groundless. And I promise you, that if any such proposition shall hereafter come, it shall not be rejected, and kept a secret

Abraham Lincoln, 1863

I thought that whatever negroes can be got to do as soldiers, leaves just so much less for white soldiers to do, in saving the Union.

from you. I freely acknowledge myself the servant of the people, according to the bond of service—the United States Constitution; and that, as such, I am responsible to them.

But to be plain, you are dissatisfied with me about the negro. Quite likely there is a difference of opinion between you and myself upon that subject. I certainly wish that all men could be free, while I suppose you do not. Yet I have neither adopted, nor proposed any measure, which is not consistent with even your view, provided you are for the Union. I suggested compensated emancipation; to which you replied you wished not to be taxed to buy negroes. But I had not asked you to be taxed to buy negroes, except in such way, as to save you from greater taxation to save the Union exclusively by other means.

You dislike the emancipation proclamation; and, perhaps, would have it retracted. You say it is unconstitutional—I think differently. I think the constitution invests its Commander-in-chief, with the law of war, in time of war. The most that can be said, if so much, is, that slaves are property. Is there—has there ever been—any question that by the law of war, property, both of enemies and friends, may be taken when needed? And is it not needed whenever taking it, helps us, or hurts the *enemy? Armies, the world over, destroy enemies' property when they can not use it; and even destroy their own to keep it from the enemy. Civilized belligerents do all in their power to help themselves, or hurt the enemy, except a few things regarded as barbarous or cruel. Among the exceptions are the massacre of vanquished foes, and non-combatants, male and female.*

But the proclamation, as law, either is valid, or is not valid. If it is not valid, it needs no retraction. If it is valid, it can not be retracted, any more than the dead can be brought to life. Some of you profess to think its retraction would operate favorably for the Union. Why better after the retraction, than before the issue? There was more than a year and a half of trial to suppress the rebellion before the proclamation issued, the last one hundred days of which passed under an explicit notice that it was coming, unless averted by those in revolt, returning to their allegiance. The war has certainly progressed as favorably for us, since the issue of proclamation as before. I know, as fully as one can know the opinions of others, that some of the commanders of our armies in the field who have given us our most important successes believe the emancipation policy and the use of the colored troops constitute the heaviest blow yet dealt to the Rebellion, and that at least one of these important successes could not have been achieved when it was but for the aid of black soldiers. Among the commanders holding these views are some who have never had any affinity with what is called aboli-tionism or with the Republican party policies but who held them purely as military opinions. I submit these opinions as being entitled to some weight against the objections often urged that emancipation and arming the blacks are unwise as military measures and were not adopted as such in good faith.

You say you will not fight to free negroes. Some of them seem will-ing to fight for you; but, no matter. Fight you, then exclusively to save the Union. I issued the proclamation on purpose to aid you in saving the Union. Whenever you shall have conquered all resistance to the

Union, if I shall urge you to continue fighting, it will be an apt time, then, for you to declare you will not fight to free negroes.

I thought that in your struggle for the Union, to whatever extent the negroes should cease helping the enemy, to that extent it weakened the enemy in his resistance to you. Do you think differently? I thought that whatever negroes can be got to do as soldiers, leaves just so much less for white soldiers to do, in saving the Union. Does it appear otherwise to you? But negroes, like other people, act upon motives. Why should they do any thing for us, if we will do nothing for them? If they stake their lives for us, they must be prompted by the strongest motive— even the promise of freedom. And the promise being made, must be kept.

The signs look better. The Father of Waters again goes unvexed to the sea. Thanks to the great Northwest for it. Nor yet wholly to them. Three hundred miles up, they met New England, Empire, Key-stone, and Jersey, hewing their way right and left. The Sunny South too, in more colors than one, also lent a hand. On the spot, their part of the history was jotted down in black and white. The job was a great national one; and let none be banned who bore an honorable part in it. And while those who have cleared the great river may well be proud, even that is not all. It is hard to say that anything has been more bravely, and well done, than at Antietam, Murfreesboro, Gettysburg, and on many fields of lesser note. Nor must Uncle Sam's web-feet be forgotten. At all the watery margins they have been present. Not only on the deep sea, the broad bay, and the rapid river, but also up the narrow muddy bayou, and wherever the ground was a little damp, they have been, and made their tracks. Thanks to all. For the great republic—for the principle it lives by, and keeps alive—for man's vast future—thanks to all.

Peace does not appear so distant as it did. I hope it will come soon, and come to stay; and so come as to be worth the keeping in all future time. It will then have been proved that, among free men, there can be no successful appeal from the ballot to the bullet; and that they who take such appeal are sure to lose their case, and pay the cost. And then, there *will be some black men who can remember that, with silent tongue, and clenched teeth, and steady eye, and well-poised bayonnet, they have helped mankind on to this great consummation; while, I fear, there will be some white ones, unable to forget that, with malignant heart, and deceitful speech, they strove to hinder it.*

Still, let us not be over-sanguine of a speedy final triumph. Let us be quite sober. Let us diligently apply the means, never doubting that a just God, in his own good time, will give us the rightful result.

Yours very truly,
A. Lincoln

An interesting footnote: Despite Conkling's instructions not to publish any part of Lincoln's message prior to its delivery, a lengthy fragment appeared in New York on September 3, prompting this Lincoln telegram to Conkling the same day: "I am mortified this morning to find the letter to you, botched up, in the Eastern papers, telegraphed from Chicago. How did this happen?" Answer: Blame the Associated Press in Chicago!

CAPTAIN RODNEY R. CHASTANT TO HIS PARENTS,

Vietnam, October 19, 1967,

Vietnam War

This tender, self-assured letter, written by Captain Rodney R. Chastant to his parents in Mobile, Alabama, deftly refers to an expression made famous by President Woodrow Wilson in his declaration of war against Germany on April 2, 1917: "The world must be made safe for democracy. . . . Civilization itself seems to be in the balance." Such arguments were not lost on the public—while some felt these words were an idealistic "mission statement," others considered the speech an example of America's ideological imperialism. For Chastant, who served with Marine Air Group 13, 1st Marine Air Wing at Da Nang, the fallen soldiers of past wars had also fought "to make the world safe for ice skating, department stores and lamp shades." He did not mean this as a joke; as his letter attests, "They are vitally important to me." Although Chastant's 13-month tour in Vietnam ended in September 1968, he volunteered to stay on for another six months. He was killed in action on October 22, 1968, at the age of 25.

Mom and Dad –

Your oldest son is now a captain in the United States Marine Corps. I was promoted yesterday. Of all the men selected for captain, 1,640 men, only about 50 men have been promoted to date. I was one of the 50, to my surprise and pleasure. My effective date of rank is 1 July 1967, which means I have technically been a captain for 3 1/2 months. I am thus due back pay for 3 1/2 months. With this promotion, my annual income is $9,000.00 a year. I'm single, 24 years old, college-educated, a captain in the Marine Corps, and I have $11,000.00 worth of securities. That is not a bad start in life, is it?

As I understand, Dad, you were married about this point in life. There was a war going on then too. I really know very little about those

You can't understand the importance these "trivial" events take on out here. It helps keep me civilized. . . . It is great to know your family's safe, living in a secure country; a country made secure by thousands upon thousands of men who have died for that country.

years in my parents' lives. Sometime you will have to tell me about them—what you were doing, what you were thinking, what you were planning, what you were hoping.

Mom, I appreciate all your letters. I appreciate your concern that some of the things you write about are trivial, but they aren't trivial to me. I'm eager to read anything about what you are doing or the family is doing. You can't understand the importance these "trivial" events take on out here. It helps keep me civilized. For a while, as I read your letters, I am a normal person. I'm not killing people, or worried about being killed. While I read your letters, I'm not carrying guns and grenades. Instead I am going ice skating with David or walking through a department store to exchange a lamp shade. It is great to know your family's safe, living in a secure country; a country made secure by thousands upon thousands of men who have died for that country.

In the Philippines I took a bus ride along the infamous route of the death march in Bataan. I passed graveyards that were marked with row after row of plain white crosses. Thousands upon thousands. These were American graves—American graves in the Philippines. And I thought about the American graves in Okinawa, Korea, France, England, North Africa—around the world. And I was proud to be an American, proud to be a Marine, proud to be fighting in Asia. I have a commitment to the men who have gone before me, American men who made the sacrifices that were required to make the world safe for ice skating, department stores and lamp shades.

No, Mom, these things aren't trivial to me. They are vitally important to me. Those are the truly important things, not what I'm doing. I hope you will continue to write about those "trivial" things because that is what I enjoy learning about the most.

Your son,
Rod

THEODORE CONLEY

War of the Philippine Insurrection

Spain was compelled to cede the Philippines (along with Puerto Rico and Guam) to the United States as a result of the Spanish-American War in 1898. That conflict stemmed from Spain's determination to suppress Cuban independence and the United States' desire to rid the hemisphere of foreigners—partly on humanitarian grounds, but also for religious and economic reasons. Spanish authority, however, was soon replaced by American influence. Commodore George Dewey's annihilation of the Spanish fleet at Manila was America's initial foothold in that island territory. With its acquisition, the United States unfortunately became an impediment to the Filipinos' own desire for independence. The Philippine Insurrection from 1899 to 1902 involved more than 120,000 U.S. troops, some of whom felt like Theodore Conley from Kansas. In an early example of using soldiers' letters for political purposes, the Anti-Imperialist League published Conley's letter in a pamphlet entitled *Soldiers' Letters, Being Materials for a History of a War of Criminal Aggression*. The noted historian Jim Zwick observes that the publication "was immediately controversial. Supporters of the

American troops and Moro tribesmen in the Philippines

war discounted the accounts of atrocities as the boasting of soldiers wanting to impress their friends and families at home or, because the identities of some of the writers were withheld from publication, as outright fabrications." The "Indians" referred to in the letter are the rebelling Philippine Moro tribesmen.

Talk about dead Indians [Moros]! Why, they are lying everywhere. The trenches are full of them. . . . More harrowing still: think of the brave men from this country, men who were willing to sacrifice their lives for the freedom of Cuba, dying in battle and from disease, in a war waged for the purpose of conquering a people who are fighting as the Cubans fought against Spanish tyranny and misrule. There is not a fea-

ture of the whole miserable business that a patriotic American citizen, one who loves to read of the brave deeds of the American colonists in the splendid struggle for American independence, can look upon with complacency, much less with pride. This war is reversing history. It places the American people and the government of the United States in the position occupied by Great Britain in 1776. It is an utterly causeless and defenseless war, and it should be abandoned by this government without delay. The longer it is continued, the greater crime it becomes—a crime against human liberty as well as against Christianity and civilization. . . . Those not killed in the trenches were killed when they tried to come out. . . . No wonder they can't shoot, with that light thrown on them; shells bursting and infantry pouring in lead all the time. Honest to God, I feel sorry for them.

MAJOR GENERAL WILLIAM T. SHERMAN TO THE ATLANTA MAYOR AND CITY COUNCIL,

Headquarters, Atlanta, Georgia, September 12, 1864, Civil War

One of the Civil War's greatest and most feared generals, William Tecumseh Sherman, was born in 1820 in Lancaster, Ohio. A graduate of West Point in 1840, he joined the Union army in 1861, developing a reputation as an aggressive and fearless leader. However, his criticism of Union strategy and an unwise boast that he could finish the war with a force of 200,000 men was widely reported in the press, which labeled him "crazy" and "insane," and the incident damaged his reputation. Sherman's career achieved a turnaround under Ulysses S. Grant. Following General Grant's specific order to "create havoc and destruction of all resources that would be beneficial to the enemy," Sherman was appointed commander of the Military Division of the Mississippi. By early May 1864, with nearly 100,000 troops behind him, he spearheaded the Atlanta campaign, aiming at the heart of the South. Four months later, after a series of unrelenting engagements, Sherman and his army forced Confederate general Hood's troops to abandon Atlanta, Georgia, and the mayor, James Calhoun, surrendered the city on September 2, 1864.

On September 11, the mayor and two councilmen pleaded with General Sherman to revoke his order for a total evacuation of their city: "We know your mind and time are constantly occupied with the duties of your command, which almost deters us from asking your attention to this matter, but we thought it might be that you had not considered this subject in all of its awful consequences, and that on more reflection you, we hope, would not make this people an exception to all mankind, for we know that no such instance ever having occurred—surely never in the United States—and what has this *helpless* people done, that they should be driven from their homes, to wander strangers and outcasts and exiles and to subsist on charity? We do not know as yet the number of people still here; of those who are here, we are satisfied a respectable number, if allowed to remain at home, could subsist for several months without assistance, and a respectable number for a much longer time, and who might not need assistance at any time. In conclusion, we most earnestly and solemnly petition you to reconsider this order, or modify it, and suffer this unfortunate people to remain at home and enjoy what little means they have." Here is Sherman's reply.

Gentlemen: I have your letter of the 11th, in the nature of a petition to revoke my orders removing all the inhabitants from Atlanta. I have read it carefully, and give full credit to your statements of the distress that will be occasioned, any yet shall not revoke my orders, because they were not designed to meet the humanities of the case, but to prepare for the future struggles in which millions of good people outside of Atlanta have a deep interest. We must have peace, *not only at Atlanta, but in all America. To secure this, we must stop the war that now desolates our once happy and favored country. To stop war, we must defeat the rebel armies which are now arrayed against the laws and*

William Tecumseh Sherman

Constitution that all must respect and obey. To defeat those armies, we must prepare the way to reach them in their recesses, provided with the arms and instruments which enable us to accomplish our purpose. Now I know the vindictive nature of our enemy, that we may have many years of military operations from this quarter; and, therefore, deem it wise and prudent to prepare in time. The use of Atlanta for warlike purposes is inconsistent with its character as a home for families. There will be no manufactures, commerce, or agriculture here, for the maintenance of families, and sooner or later want will compel the inhabitants to go. Why not go now, when all the arrangements are completed for the transfer, instead of waiting till the plunging shot of contending armies will renew the scenes of the past month? Of course, I do not apprehend any such thing at this moment, but you do not suppose this army will be here until the war is over. I cannot discuss this subject with you fairly, because I cannot impart to you what we propose to do, but I assert that our military plans make it necessary for the inhabitants to go away, and I can only renew my offer of services to make their exodus in any direction as easy and comfortable as possible.

You cannot qualify war in harsher terms than I will. War is cruelty, and you cannot refine it; and those who brought war into our country deserve all the curses and maledictions a people can pour out. I know I had no hand in making this war, and I know I will make more sacrifices to-day than any of you to secure peace. But you cannot have peace and a division of our country. If the United States submits to a division now, it will not stop, but will go on until we reap the fate of Mexico, which is eternal war. The United States does and must assert its authority, wherever it once had power; for, if it relaxes one bit to pressure, it is gone, and I believe that such is the national feeling. This feeling assumes various shapes, but always comes back to that of Union. Once admit the Union, once more acknowledge the authority of the national Government, and, instead of devoting your houses and streets and roads to the dread uses of war, I and this army become at once your protectors

and supporters, shielding you from danger, let it come from what quar-
ter it may. I know that a few individuals cannot resist a torrent of error
and passion, such as swept the South into rebellion, but you can point
out, so that we may know those who desire a government, and those who
insist on war and its desolation.

You might as well appeal against the thunder-storm as against
these terrible hardships of war. They are inevitable, and the only way
the people of Atlanta can hope once more to live in peace and quiet at
home, is to stop the war, which can only be done by admitting that it
began in error and is perpetuated in pride.

We don't want your Negroes, or your horses, or your houses, or your
hands, or any thing you have, but we do want and will have a just obe-
dience to the laws of the United States. That we will have, and if it
involves the destruction of your improvements, we cannot help it.

You have heretofore read public sentiment in your newspapers, that
live by falsehood and excitement; and the quicker you seek for truth in
other quarters, the better. I repeat then that, by the original compact of
government, the United States had certain rights in Georgia, which have
never been relinquished and never will be; that the South began the war
by seizing forts, arsenals, mints, custom-houses, etc., etc., long before Mr.
Lincoln was installed, and before the South had one jot or title of provo-
cation. I myself have seen in Missouri, Kentucky, Tennessee, and
Mississippi, hundreds and thousands of women and children fleeing from
your armies and desperadoes, hungry and with bleeding feet. In Memphis,
Vicksburg, and Mississippi, we fed thousands upon thousands of families
of rebel soldiers left on our hands, and whom we could not see starve.
Now that war comes home to you, you feel very different. You depreci-
ate its horrors, but did not feel them when you sent car-loads of soldiers
and ammunition, and moulded shells and shot, to carry war into
Kentucky and Tennessee, to desolate the homes of hundreds of thousands
of good people who only asked to live in peace at their old homes, and
under the Government of their inheritance. But these comparisons are

idle. I want peace, and believe it can only be reached through union and war, and I will ever conduct war with a view to perfect and early success.

But, my dear sirs, when peace does come, you may call on me for any thing. Then I will share with you the last cracker, and watch with you to shield your homes and families against danger from every quarter.

Now you must go, and take with you the old and feeble, feed and nurse them, and build for them, in more quiet places, proper habitations to shield them against the weather until the mad passions of men cool down, and allow the Union and peace once more to settle over your old homes at Atlanta. Yours in haste,

W. T. Sherman, Major-General commanding

Sherman's forces remained in Atlanta until November, at which time he began his infamous March to the Sea. Before his evacuation, he ordered the burning of any installation that could still be useful to the Confederacy—unfortunately, the fire got out of control and much of the city was destroyed, an event that Sherman regretted for the rest of his life. In a speech he reportedly made before the graduating class of the Michigan Military Academy in 1879 (but first published in 1914) Sherman remarked, "I am tired and sick of War. Its glory is all moonshine. It is only those who have never fired a shot nor heard the shrieks and groans of the wounded who cry aloud for blood, more vengeance, more desolation. War is hell."

From the Front

CONFEDERATE PRIVATE
ISAAC HOWARD TO HIS FATHER,

camp near Fredericksburg, Virginia,

December 25, 1862,

Civil War

I n 1862, President Lincoln appointed General Ambrose Burnside head of the Army of the Potomac. Anxious to capitalize on Union victories, but moving too cautiously, Burnside lost an opportunity to divide and defeat Confederate general Lee's forces stationed along the Rappahannock near Fredericksburg, Virginia. The North's poorly designed and executed river crossings during the ensuing Fredericksburg campaign of November–December 1862 caused numerous casualties. A stone wall along Marye's Heights near the city was littered with dead and wounded Federals—and Union losses numbered nearly 13,000 against 5,300 for the Confederates. Unaware that Northern casualties were so significant, Lee chose not to take the advantage, and Burnside's army withdrew during the night of December 15. Isaac Howard survived the campaign of Fredericksburg but died six months later during the battle of Gettysburg.

> *The yankee scoundrels almost completely destroyed Fredricksburg, they vented their malice & spleen in the most wanton manner, Breaking up and destroying whatever they could not remove.*

I received your letter of the 22nd. [torn] today I was very glad indeed to [torn] home once more as it was the first h[torn] I had heard from home in nearly 4 mon[torn] I was very much relieved [sic] to hear that all were well at home. I was sorry to hear that Tom was ill all of the time that he was at home. I suppose you will have heard of the great battle of Fredricksburg before this letter reaches you. The Yankees sustained the most utter and terrible defeat, probably that they have experienced during the war. It was the most glorious victory we have ever gained, our loss is trifling in comparison with the enemy, according to Gen. Lee's report of the battle our loss was 1800 killed wounded and missing, while that of the enemy according to their own statement was 15,500, and many of their papers place it as high as 20,000. Not more than one half of our forces were engaged [torn]r brigade didn't fire a gun. Gen Lee [torn]d that we had suffered so severely—[torn] Gaines

The rifle pits in front of the Marye House in Fredericksburg

farm, Manassas No 2 and Sharps[bu]rg, and that he had called upon us so [torn]ften in tight places, that we should be held in reserve. Our regt had 5 or 6 men wounded by shell, no one was killed. I think that we will go into winter quarters soon, as the yankees seem to be disgusted with their ill success of this winters campaign, & they are said to be going back to the Potomac, to go into winter quarters.

The yankee scoundrels almost completely destroyed Fredricksburg, they vented their malice & spleen in the most wanton manner, Breaking up and destroying whatever they could not remove. Nothing was too pure or sacred for their unbridled lust. The very churches were pillaged of of whatever value or ornament they contained. The retribution they received for their iniquitous proceedings was sudden and terrible. The town was literally choked with [torn] dead. There was 5,000 dead bodies of [torn]kee soldiers lying stiffening on that [torn]d field the day after the fight. And [torn]he fight had been general throughout the whole line, the yankee army would have been nearly annihilated, as it was their army was completely demoralized and recrossed the river more like a rabble rout that the grandest army the world ever saw as the yankees were so fond of terming it. The weather for the last few days has been admirable and to day it is as mild and beautiful as any Christmas I ever remember having seen in Texas.

Tell Ma not to be the least uneasy about my personal comfort. I have plenty of good clothes and blankets and have been in excellent health ever since the fall set in.

There isn't much preparation for Christmas in camp, the boys are in excellent spirits however, not much doing in the egg-nog line, but with butter, molasses, sugar, confederated c[torn] and apples, from the sutler's, and peas[torn] roast-beef and hot biscuits from our own [torn] we managed to make out a pretty good [torn] dinner. I wish I could send some apples, nice red rosy cheeked fellows to Nellie and Susie, bless their little hearts. I am going down to see Conway sometime during the C.X. who is camped about 8 miles below here near Port Royal. I got a letter from Aunt Ellen a few days ago, all were well. I send this letter by private conveyance and will send some papers with it.

Good bye my dear father, God bless and preserve you from every danger. Give my best love to all, and to Charlie and Tom whenever you write.

Your affectionate boy

LIEUTENANT DAVID HUGHES TO CAPTAIN JOHN R. FLYNN,

at sea on the <u>Oturu Maru,</u> February 7, 1952, Korean War

★

Hughes fought in the Korean War as part of the 7th U.S. Cavalry, for which he was awarded the Distinguished Service Cross and two Silver Stars. It was Hughes's regiment, however, that was also involved in the controversial killing of civilians at No Gun Ri on July 26, 1950, brought to light in 1999 by the Associated Press. The following remarkable and descriptive letter by Lieutenant Hughes, covering the events of September and October 1951, was written on his way back to the United States from Japan. He sent it to Captain John Flynn, his first company commander, who had been wounded and sent home. Flynn returned the letter to Hughes prior to a 1995 reunion of the Korean Chapter of the 7th Cavalry. It has been edited for publication.

★

Capt. Flynn:
There is lots to say in bringing you up to date since you left. Here beside me I have several false starts on letters to you. . . . I changed jobs

at a lucky time. In the S-3 shop [regimental headquarters operations staff], I was in one the post-battle discussions and writings of the Regiment, and talked with the generals and the staffs, and read. So now I can say what there is to be said.

I learned and saw enough since you left to write ten books, all of them different. Personalities rose and fell, battles swelled and diminished, boys became men, and men became memories.

The Regiment fought like a demon for some pieces of ground and suffered incredible casualties defending it. And then, partly because of the casualties, the division was pulled out and replaced. It was time. The 1st Cav Division was left only with a smattering of real strength. . . . After you were hit, the division went back to the Kansas line and dug and wired in for a few weeks. The 25th Division had our sector. The 24th Regiment had the old 7th Cav sector and fared pretty badly. When we came back up they had lost the patrol base on the 487-477 hill mass, which the 3d Battalion had for so long. We were not to get that hill mass back until four months later after five well planned attacks—two of them regimental size—had failed. . . .

The Chinese started digging in on a line from Hill 487 in front of Hill 347 and on down to the Imjin. So we kept patrolling out farther and farther until that line was established; then we sent out the patrol bases again. That set the stage for the offensive. . . .

We were involved in one of the battles for 487. The line generally paralleled the road to from Yonchon to Chorwon, and at this time the 3d Division had the sector down to opposite 477. The 3d Battalion of the 7th was given the job of a dawn attack in a flanking move around the north and east of 487. It was up the two tough sides of the mountain, but was probably the least defended too.

We moved and jumped off on schedule; at least Company K did. Companies L and I were late, and we had seized our first objective before they reached the line of departure. But we pulled up and soon were on the two fingers. The peak and its approaches had been plastered day and night for a long time by weapons of all calibers up to 8-inch. The peak was bare, but the Chinese were too well dug in. Three thousand rounds of 4.2-inch mortars were used in preparation.

Up we went and learned the defenses were simply impregnable. On K Company's approach, the last 300 yards was a 45 degree slope, with no cover. The Chinese laced into us with five machine guns, and we were so placed that we were attacking the rim of a teacup from inside the bottom. At the high point of the attack, 200 yards from the top, the whole assaulting platoon was under direct observation on a concave slope. I had everything in the book going in at the bunkers—precision registered 155mm, direct fire from five tanks, and all the rest—but not one machinegun was silenced.

We were ordered off in late afternoon with 23 casualties, 20 of them gunshot. Company L had about the same. Two weeks later the entire 65th Regiment tried to take the peak and failed.

One of my platoon leaders was badly shot up in the arm, which left Lieutenant Radcliffe, 1st Platoon leader, and me again. But the new Company K had been blooded; the men were more ready to fight and knew what to expect.

For another couple weeks, we ran patrols from near Yonchon, and I got in five good officers. Then we watched the two patrol bases out in front of us get it in the neck. One was on Hill 343 and the other on 339. Hill 339 was key, and about halfway between lines. It was lost and gained by patrols every few days. One day Company C was sent out to hold a perimeter on it, which they did for two days and on the night of the third was completely overrun in a mass attack. We got the hill back again with the 2d battalion and then they were ordered off. This yo-yo game continued until 21 September when they ordered the 3d Battalion out to hold a patrol base from 339 to 343 and back over to 321, a 4,000 yard perimeter. . . .

We moved out and after plastering the hill from an OP [observation post] on 321, 1,500 yards away, we went up, but the Chinese set off a red flare and pulled off. I topped the peak and about five minutes afterward learned what the score was going to be for the next two weeks. They suddenly began shelling us and mortaring until I thought the roof was going to come off the hill.

They kept working the front slope over with a battery of 75mms and self-propelled artillery and they shook us to pieces with more 120mm mortars than I thought we had in 4.2-inch. The rain of 82mm and 60mm was just incidental. The fewest incoming rounds we ever reported for 24 hours was 350, and we estimated 1,200 on the second day.

It took me until the second day to see why they had targetted us while hardly touching the rest of the perimeter. Once on the peak OP, I could see more of their positions and gun positions and access routes than they could afford to have me see.

So it went. We dug in amidst dead enemy troops from earlier battles and tried to organize the hill. They watched us like hawks, though, and could see our rear slope from the flanks. We could not top the ridge or put a single man in position on the forward slope during daylight; they would just open up with the SP [self-propelled] and dig him right out of the hole. From bombardment alone, with very little movement on the hill, we took 33 casualties in a week from direct hits on holes with mortars and the midnight dose of 120's. The first night, we had a scrap. They came across a little saddle from which they had hit Company C, and they came down the road on the extreme right flank. On the road they ran into a tank, and it scattered them while the mortar fire kept them dispersed. But on the peak they plastered us with everything they could, and came in right under their own mortar fire to hit the right shoulder of the hill and smack into Sergeant Malloy's machinegun. He waited until they were ten yards away and then cut loose. They did not definitely locate him in the confusion and noise, and he stopped them cold. They crawled around and poured machinegun fire on us for a few more hours and then pulled off their dead and with-

drew. In the morning there were five dead enemy within those ten yards of Malloy, and one had his hand draped over the parapet. We took no casualties from the small arms. . . .

We sent out daily patrols that only got 600 yards before getting hit. On the 25th, I had to send out a platoon toward positions I knew were there. I didn't like it at all because the enemy had been get cagier and cagier and had been holding their fire. But out went Lt. Radcliffe and his 1st Platoon. The Chinese let them get 200 yards from the peak before opening up with cross-firing weapons. Radcliffe was killed instantly. The platoon sergeant, a corporal, didn't hesitate. He ordered marching fire, and the platoon took half the peak so the rest could get out. There were three dead. Sergeant Brown was cut down by a grenade near Radcliffe. He rolled over and took Radcliffe's .45 pistol and the maps and took them all back as he himself was carried out. A machinegunner who could not find a vantage point to set up his machinegun went up with it cradled in his arm with one belt of ammunition. He had to be evacuated for the burns on his arm.

Every night, enemy patrols would crawl up and feel us out. They plotted our weapons and counted our men. Every night I would have to get up and calm down a squad that thought the whole Chinese Army was out there. But this had one good effect. The men dug in tight. They kept their weapons spotless. They slept in the daytime and watched at night. The 60mm mortar crew got faster and faster under colored platoon leader Lieutenant Walker. I collected heavy machineguns and on the 28th had five heavies and seven lights across the front. But because of the fire and dwindling number of men, we had been able to put out only a few rolls of concertina wire on the two easy approaches. The engineers all but refused to work laying mines in front of us.

The night of the 28th came. The day had been quiet and it seemed as good a time as any for the big show.

At 2330 a bombardment came in. It was deadly accurate and concentrated on the positions controlling the two approaches. It continued until 2400 and then, for a few minutes, stepped up to a frenzied firing of all kinds of shells.

Then . . . all hell broke loose. A company hit each flank, and even with the 4.2's dropping right in the draw they came up, they overran the tie-in with Company L and rolled up the flank of the understrength 1st Platoon. On the right they were stopped for a while by the automatic weapons and the 81mm and 60mm mortars, but there again they punched through a squad front and overran that squad turning toward the peak through the 2d Platoon. Not a man bugged out, and all our dead soldiers in the morning were found in their holes.

By this time, all the defensive fires were going full blast, but I was waiting for the Sunday punch. It came in about 20 minutes later at 0110. The Chinese only had a strip of our territory about 150 yards long on the right and 200 yards on the left, but they sure filled it up. They moved a mortar onto the ridge of each flank and began peppering the CP [command post]. They got a couple of machineguns up there and fired overhead for their next attack. And they never stopped pounding the top of the hill with those 120s. Then they jumped off again. The Chinese companies that had penetrated sent people around behind us, and they raked the back slope with small arms and cut off our communications with battalion.

I did not know this at the time, but two things had happened. One was that they had attacked neatly, the first time, just to the left of the two machineguns on the right flank and thus never touched any part of the 3d Platoon. Only two rifle platoons were involved all night long! The second thing was that at the beginning of the attack, the battalion S-2 [intelligence] section had been monitoring the SCR 300 [captured US radio] stations, and their Chinese interpreter picked up the command channel of the battalion that was attacking my company. So all night long battalion headquarters had a running account of the battle and knew how we stood, from the talk on the company radios the Chinese used and their command radio.

That was the high point of the attack.... The reserve heavy machine-gun had done its work, but its water cans were full of holes. Our urine had run out, but a can of cold coffee lasted the rest of the night.

When the big attack came at 0110, the two companies on the ridgeline on both flanks started the attack toward the peak. Just when they were exerting maximum pressure on the heavy machineguns at the shoulder of the peak on each flank, two more companies came at us on those two saddle approaches we had wired in. I was waiting for that, and on the left, as they started across the wire, we opened up with the 57mm [recoilless rifle] at 20 yards on the wire, and I called in the 155s at a range of 150 yards from us and the two fires caught the company on the move.

On the right they attacked across that little saddle, and we were waiting there too. At the first sign of the attack I called in the 4.2 mortar fire to 125 yards, and it played havoc with the supporting troops. I started the 60mm mortars firing at top speed (by this time we were getting artillery flares) and then, as the first grenade throwing wave hit our positions, we turned on the two flame throwers. The first wave just expired (fried) where it was. In a short time we were out of flame thrower juice, but it had scared them and the next waves walked across instead of running. I kept dropping the 60mm fire closer and closer until we went to 83 degrees—firing nearly vertically—when firing on a gun to target range of 65 yards and we were dropping shells only 15 yards in front of the machinegunner. It finally broke them, but only after they had got the 2d Platoon CP and had the platoon backed up to our mortar position.

On the left they got much closer. They killed the crew of one of our heavy machinegun sections, broke through the refused flank, and came steaming up the hill at our CP about 35 yards up. I had every man I could spare on the perimeter, including the 5th Platoon (South Koreans) which did good work that night, so I asked my personal radio operator to commit the reserve. That consisted of one heavy machinegun that was sitting on top of my CP bunker. He set it up and stopped the attack 15 yards from the CP, which was full of wounded. Then I sent my first sergeant to the 57mm recoilless rifle section, which was now in an untenable position. As the section soldiers came up the hill a Chinese soldier came up with them, and after a tussle was killed in the CP.

I shot him with my submachine gun after he jumped into the hole with me.

That was the high point of the attack. They had captured three of our men on the left. One of them they took off the hill immediately; the second and third were pushed up in front of them toward us during the attack, but one—seeing that heavy machinegun kill all of their mortar crew and cut down on the attack wave—kicked his captor, jumped over the side of the steep ridge, and escaped. The third GI went on up and was killed by our fire. . . .

The reserve heavy machinegun had done its work, but its water cans were full of holes. Our urine had run out, but a can of cold coffee lasted the rest of the night.

*The enemy radios had reported that three of their company com-
manders had been killed and they could not get the GIs off the hill.
They asked permission to withdraw but were told they had to have the
hill "tonight." Then the reserve company, the fifth one, claimed they
had so many wounded from the artillery that they could not carry them
back and therefore could not attack. Of course we didn't know any of
this.*

*Then our Regimental Commander hailed a flight of B-26s, and
under flare light and by radar they dive bombed the ridge 600 yards in
front of us. We drew up in a tight perimeter at 0430 and waited out
the day. In the morning we cleared the flanks and bombarded many
enemy trying to flee over the hills with their wounded and dead.*

*We still could not move around very well, because the enemy fire
was still coming in, but by 0800 we counted 77 dead within our positions. We had suffered 10 killed, 15 wounded, and 1 captured.*

*We were pretty beat up by this time, having taken—with attach-
ments—54 casualties in the seven days on Hill 339. On the 29th, we
were rotated around the battalion perimeter and Company I took over.*

[Hughes continues to describe another period of harrowing
attacks, and concludes his letter with:]

*And that's how we were when the division went into reserve, and
got ready to ship out to Japan. The 1st Cavalry Division had taken a
real pounding; it never suffered more casualties in an equal period during its tour in Korea. Company K, which ran about fifth in casualties,
lost 167 men and 6 officers. But we won all our battles.*

*Although I held down a captain's vacancy for six and a half months
straight, the Army did not promote me, so I am still a first lieutenant.
But I am on my way home and hope to see you soon.*

Lt. David Hughes

PRIVATE DENNIS FORD
TO HIS WIFE AND NEIGHBORS,
Washington, D.C., September 6, 1862,
Civil War

On December 17, 1861, Dennis Ford, a 38-year-old laborer from Haverhill, enlisted in the nearly all-Irish 28th Massachusetts, known as the "Faugh-A-Ballaugh Regiment" (Gaelic for "clear the way"). The Irish Brigade, which fought bravely at Marye's Heights' Stone Wall, was part of the 1st Division, II Corps, Army of the Potomac. The 28th first saw action in June 1862, during skirmishes on James Island and, two weeks later, during the attack on Fort Johnson (known as the Battle of Secessionville). Its first major engagement was at Second Bull Run, but Ford's letter refers to the fighting at Chantilly (or Ox Hill), Virginia, on September 1, 1862. The Irish Brigade's combined losses during the war were nearly 1,000 dead and 3,000 wounded, with the 28th losing 250 of its 800 men.

Dear Wife and Neighbors,

I am living still, thank God. I been in four battles since I left Newport News. We had two severe ones. We lost half our regiment. The last fight, my clothes were riddled with balls. I was grazed in the right arm. It knocked my arm dead, though thank God I have not seen one drop of blood as yet. The rubber blanket I had on my back was riddled. A ball struck me on the shoe. They fell around me like hail. James Phillips is shot dead. The rest of the boys are safe. John Maher was wounded. Peter King got something like a wound, it is nothing. John Fenning was wounded. Con Roach came out safe. Maurice and the Donnellys are safe. We lost in the last fight 130 men out of our regiment.

It would be too tedious for me to tell what I went through—the long marching for the last 26 days. Half hungry, some would kill cows and skin a part of them, cut off a piece and waste it, and never open them. Some would shoot pigs and sheep, and would never open them, only cut a piece and roast it and leave the rest behind. Some would carry their coffee in their hand and march in the ranks and drink it, some would spill it. Sometimes, the dinner and breakfast would be cooking, they would get word to march, they would have to spill it and throw it away and march. The rebels fare worse than we do.

Let me know how are the children. Let me know about the note. I did not receive an answer to the last letter I wrote you from Newport News. Write as soon as you receive this, as we don't know the hour we will be on the march.

The war is raging in every direction the rebels fight in the woods. So I must conclude. Give my best love and respects to all the friends and neighbors. Let me know how times are in Haverhill. We received no pay for the last two months. When you write, let me know all the particulars. Our priest can't stand the hardship, we fear he will leave though he is a smart young man. They treat him very bad.

So I must conclude. Do pray for us, we look shabby and thin, though we were called a clean regiment. I saw a great deal shot and wounded. Balls drove through their [lines]. The 28th Mass. suffered [along with] the 79th New York. Our regiment stood the severest fire that was witnessed. During the war, when we got into the woods, we ran through what we did not shoot. We bayoneted them. One man begged and got no mercy, a yankee ran him through. Thank God it was not an Irishman did it.

So I must conclude. I remain your humble husband Dennis Ford until death. I am in hopes I will see Haverhill once more before I die with the help of God. Direct to Washington, to me, Company H, 28 Regiment Mass. Vol. Tell Mrs. McCormick her friend Thomas Cline is well. There was one James Short from Lawrence [who] fell in the last battle.

After the Union's defeat at Second Bull Run, the 28th Massachusetts retreated to Washington. In the campaign that followed, the regiment left camp at Meridian Hill on September 7 and marched with McClellan's army until reaching Turner's Gap on September 14. Three days later, the 28th participated in the ferocious Battle of Antietem, at which time three of the men Ford reported alive in his letter were killed. Ford, later listed as missing in action at Gettysburg, returned to Company H until his capture at Charles City Cross Roads, Virginia, on August 16, 1864. He was part of a prisoner exchange three months later, and discharged on December 19, 1864.

(Opposite): Soldiers from the Irish Brigade at Harrison's Landing

2ND LIEUTENANT CHARLES W. LARNED TO HIS MOTHER,

7th Cavalry, Camp on the Musselshell River,

August 19, 1873, U.S.-Indian Wars

On July 28, 1866, George Armstrong Custer, who had served as a general in the Civil War, was appointed lieutenant colonel of the newly formed 7th Cavalry. In March 1873, his regiment was ordered to the Great Plains to escort surveyors working on the Northern Pacific Railroad. The company, under the leadership of financier Jay Cooke, had been awarded a tract totaling 39 million acres on which to build a railway line from Duluth to Puget Sound. Despite an 1868 treaty barring them, settlers had entered the Sioux ancestral lands and hunting grounds of the Black Hills in the Dakota Territory, lured by the promise of Dakota gold. Custer fought several skirmishes against the Sioux in early August as the caravan of 275 supply wagons, 373 civilians, and 1,500 soldiers traversed the Wyoming and Montana territories.

Dr. John Hensinger, veterinary surgeon, Seventh Cavalry, and Mr. Balaran, sutler [a provisioner to the army], were [on August 4] the two

> *For three hours the fight was kept up. . . . After this desultory fighting had become tiresome, the cavalry mounted suddenly and dashed forward at a charge, scattering their wary antagonists . . .*

victims to a want of caution that our long immunity from attack had engendered They had left the train during the halt for the purpose of watering their horses, and on their way back skirting the foot of the bluffs in order to meet the column in its descent, quite unconscious of danger and the horrible fate awaiting them, were suddenly surprised by a party of three Sioux, who had secreted themselves in a ravine, and shot from behind with arrows.

General Custer in the morning had taken a squadron, A and B troops of the Seventh Cavalry, and moved rapidly ahead of the main body about four miles beyond the point at which this tragedy occurred. There, in a belt of woods, his escort had unsaddled, picketed their horses and were lying under the trees awaiting the arrival of the main body, when a shot from the pickets and their sudden appearance brought everyone to his feet. Quickly and quietly the horses were brought in and saddled, a dismounted detachment thrown out as skirmishers, while the remainder of the command moved in the direction of the attack. But three or four Indians were to be seen, galloping and gesticulating wildly *in front of the column, which moved quickly forward at a trot. Hardly, however, had the flank arrived opposite a second belt of dense woods before a long line of Indians suddenly moved in regular orders from their midst straight to the attack. They were all in full war costume, mounted on stalwart little ponies, and armed, as are all we have seen, with the best of Henry rifles. As rapidly as possible the command was dismounted and formed in skirmish line in front of the horses, but not a moment too soon, as the enemy came whooping and screeching down upon it. A square volley in their teeth cooled their ardor, and sent them flying back to a respectful distance. For three hours the fight was kept up, the Indians maintaining a perfect skirmish line throughout, and evincing for them a very extraordinary control and discipline. After this desultory fighting had become tiresome, the cavalry mounted suddenly and dashed forward at a charge, scattering their wary antagonists, who were not prepared for such a demonstration, in every direction. Our casualties were one man and three horses wounded. The loss of the enemy, estimated from those seen to fall, must have been something in the vicinity of ten in all, and five ponies.*

For the next three days nothing was seen of our friendly neighbors in person, but abundant evidence of their camps, and the heavy trail of a retreating village, numbering, as our Indian scouts told us, in the neighborhood of eighty lodges. Each day General Custer, with two squadrons of cavalry, pushed on in advance, following rapidly on the trail.

It was not, however, until the evening of August 8 that he received orders from General Stanley to push on with the whole of the available cavalry force, make forced night marches, and overtake the village, if possible . . .

At early dawn on the 10th our efforts to cross [the Tongue River] commenced, and it was not until 4 in the afternoon that they were reluctantly relinquished, after every expedient had been resorted to in vain. The current was too swift and fierce for our heavy cavalry. We

FROM THE FRONT ★45★

therefore went into bivouac close to the riverbank to await the arrival of the main body, and slept that night as only men in such condition can sleep. We hardly anticipated the lively awakening that awaited us. Just at daylight our slumbers were broken by a sharp volley of musketry from the opposite bank, accompanied by shouts and yells that brought us all to our feet in an instant. As far up the river as we could see, clouds of dust announced the approach of our slippery foes, while the rattling volleys from the opposite woods, and the "zip," "zip" of the balls about our ears told us that there were a few evil-disposed persons close by.

For half an hour, while the balls flew high, we lay still without replying, but when the occasional quiver of a wounded horse told that the range was being acquired by them, the horses and men were moved back from the river edge to the foot of the bluffs, and there drawn up in line of battle to await developments. A detachment of sharpshooters was concealed in the woods, and soon sent back a sharp reply to the thickening compliments from the other side. Our scouts and the Indians were soon exchanging chaste complimentary remarks in choice Sioux—such as: "We're coming over to give you h—;" "You'll see more Indians than you ever saw before in your life," and "Shoot, you son of a dog" from ours. Sure enough, over they came, as good as their word, above and below us, and in twenty minutes our scouts came tumbling down the bluffs head overheels, screeching; "Heap Indian come." Just at this moment General Custer rode up to the line, followed by a bright guidon [a military flag], and made rapid disposition for the defense. Glad were we that the moment of action had arrived, and that we were to stand no longer quietly and grimly in line of battle to be shot at. One platoon of the first squadron on the left was moved rapidly up the bluffs, and thrown out in skirmish line on the summit, to hold the extreme left. The remainder of the squadron followed as quickly as it could be deployed, together with one troop of the Fourth Squadron.

On they came as before, 500 or 600 in number, screaming and yelling as usual, right onto the line before they saw it. At the same *moment the regimental band, which had been stationed in a ravine just in rear, struck up "GarryOwen" [the seventh Cavalry's official marching song]. The men set up a responsive shout, and a rattling volley swept the whole line.*

Our scouts and the Indians were soon exchanging chaste complimentary remarks in choice Sioux—such as: "We're coming over to give you h—;"... and "Shoot, you son of a dog"

The fight was short and sharp just here, the Indians rolling back after the first fire and shooting from a safer distance. In twenty minutes the squadrons were mounted and ordered to charge. Our evil-disposed friends tarried no longer, but fled incontinently before the pursuing squadrons. We chased them eight miles and over the river, only returning when the last Indian had gotten beyond our reach.

No less than a thousand warriors had surrounded us, and we could see on the opposite bluffs the scattered remnants galloping wildly to and fro. Just at the conclusion of the fight the infantry came up, and two shells from the Rodman guns completed the discomfiture of our demoralized foes. Our loss was one killed, Private Tuttle, E Troop, Seventh Cavalry, and three wounded. Among the latter, Lieutenant [Charles] Braden, Seventh Cavalry, while gallantly holding the extreme left, the hottest portion of the line, was shot through the thigh, crushing the bone badly. Four horses were killed and eight or ten wounded, and deserve honorable mention, although noncombatants. Official estimates place the Indian loss at forty killed and wounded, and a large number of ponies.

Speculation in railroads caused Jay Cooke's Northern Pacific Railroad to collapse during the panic of 1873, forcing the company to sell its landholdings to pay off stockholders. The 7th Cavalry suffered a more deadly setback of its own: Just three years later, on June 25, 1876, Custer and his men made their last stand against the Sioux near the Little Bighorn River, less than 100 miles from where Larned's letter was written.

2ND LIEUTENANT STEWART A. MELNICK TO HIS UNCLE DAVID RAAB

Vietnam, April 28, 1968,
Vietnam War

S tewart Melnick, from Bradley Beach, New Jersey, served with the 9th Infantry after attending Officer Candidate School at Fort Bragg, North Carolina. His vivid letter underscores not just his bravery and his commitment to his men and country, but also reveals the blunt—if not brutal—reality that innocents are killed in combat and soldiers sometimes die because other soldiers fail to save them. Known to his men as "Spunky" for his bright and outgoing nature, Melnick writes to his uncle that if he must "express [himself] to someone really bad," he is relieved he can, but he'll "try not to make a habit of it." The boy who looked forward to home-baked chocolate chip cookies was the same man who looked down into the face of his dying buddy. Melnick's letter does not express remorse, but there is anger and resignation along with a sense of exhilaration and pride. One senses, however, that an acknowledgment of remorse or sorrow might have left him open to doubts about his mission.

(Opposite): A soldier from the 9th Infantry in My Tho, Vietnam

Dear Dave,

How are you, Helen and the kids? I'm fine and working toward my fourth month in country now. Things are pretty active in the Delta area I'm in. The other night I ambushed a truck that ran through two roadblocks prior to comming to my location. I blew the damn thing off the road. In it were three men, one woman and a child. After the occurrance it turned out the men were VC but the woman and kid were innocent. Anyway it didn't matter to them too much after it was all over. I don't think they even realized what hit them. We've been having some rough times with booby traps lately. And I expect that they'll be more frequent now that monsoons have arrived. Since the VC can't move too much in the rainy season he tries to hamper the Americans movement by setting more traps. Luckily I have three pointmen who know their job good enough to avoid and detect most of the traps. The rest of them . . . well thats life.

So far two of my boys have been killed and about 15 wouned. And I'm lucky thats all because somedays we just seem to catch all the hell Charlie throws out. This includes ambushes and traps to sniper fire and landing in the hot LZ's (Landing Zones) when we travel by choppers. Although most of my day is taken up and I'm confronted with beaucoup problems, I wouldn't trade places with anyone in this G-d forsaken world. Its the greatest challenge that I've ever experienced and being so near living death makes one realize just how much life is worth.

I agree that we belong here but I don't agree with the policy by which we fight this war. It dawns on you when you are pinned down for six hours under heavy fire and can't bring in a dust-off (medical Helicopter) to extract a wounded buddy. And Bang, there you are, stuck to watch him die before you. I had cleared the blood from his nasal passages and beat his chest furiously but he couldn't make it because the will to live without an eye and leg was too much to bear. Babe, I couldn't care less how I come home just so long as I still could remember that there are *beaucoup* things to live for and believe me relatives like you are enough for me to fight for my life.

You told me once that if I had to express myself to someone really bad that you were the ones I could write them to. I'll try not to make a habit of it though.

So far I was wounded twice and treated myself both times. Once on my chest and the second one is on the left side of my face by the side of my eye. It makes me look tough like John Garfield and I'm sort of proud of it even though its only a small scar.

O.K. Helen you put your foot in your own mouth. I want home backed chocolate chip cookies. Put that in your pipe and smoke it. I think in about another two months I'll be going to the 101st Airborne Division. I'm trying like hell to get a transfer there and some good word has come down already. When I get back to the states next February I should be going back to Special Forces.

Give my love to the kids and Mrs. Liebowitz. I pray that shes feeling fine. G-d bless you.

As Ever,
Stew

Melnick, who was awarded the Purple Heart, the Bronze Star, the Silver Star, and the Vietnamese Medal of Honor, was scheduled to return to the States in June 1969. He was killed in action on September 3, 1968, while leading a combat mission in the Mekong Delta. At his battalion's memorial service in Vietnam, he was eulogized with the words, "I thank my God upon every remembrance of you."

28 Apr 68

Dear Dave,

How are you, Helen and the kids? I'm fine and working toward my fourth month in country now. Things are pretty active in the Delta area I'm in. The other night I ambushed a truck that ran through two roadblocks prior to comming to my location. I blew the damn thing off the road. In it were three men, one woman and a child. After the occurrance it turned out the men were VC but the woman and kid were innocent. Anyway it didn't matter to them too much after it was all over. I don't think they even realized what hit them. We've been having some rough times with booby traps lately. And I expect that they'll be more frequent now that monsoons have arrived. Since the VC can't move too much in the rainy season he tries to hamper the Americans movement by setting more traps. Luckily I have three pointmen who know their job good enough to avoid and detect most of the traps. The rest of them... well thats life.

So far two of my boys have been killed and about 15 wouned. And I'm lucky thats all because somedays we just seem to catch all the hell Charlie throws out. This includes ambushes and traps to sniper fire and landing in hot LZ's (Landing Zones) when we travel by choppers. Although most of my day is taken up and I'm confronte d with beaucoup problems, I wouldn't trade places with anyone in this G-d forsaken world. Its the greatest challenge that I've ever experienced and being so near living death makes one realize just how much life is worth.

I agree that we belong here but I don't agree with the policy by which we fight this war. It dawns on you when you are pinned down for six hours under heavy fire and can't bring in a dust-off (medical Helicopter) to extract a wounded buddy. And Bang, there you are , stuck to watch him die before you. I had cleared the bblood from his nasal passages and beat on his chest furiously but he couldn't make it because the will to live without an eye and leg was too much to bear. Babe, I couldu't care less how I come home just so long as I still could remember that there are beaucoup things to live for and believe me relatives like you are enough for me to fight for my life.

You told me once that if I had to express myself to someone really bad that you were the ones I could write them to. I'll try not to make a habit of it though.

So far I was wounded twice and treated myself both times. Once on my chest and the second one is on the left side of my face by the side of my eye. It makes me look tough like John Garfield and I'm sort of proud of it even though its only a small scar.

O.K. Helen you put your foot in your own mouth. I want home backed chocolate chip cookies. Put that in your pipe and smoke it. I think in about another two months I'll be going to the 101st Airborne Division. I'm trying like hell to transfer there and some good word has come down already. When I get back to the states next February I should be going back to Special Forces.

Give my love to the kids and Mrs. Liebowitz. I pray that shes feeling fine. G-d bless you

As Ever

Stew

FRIEDRICH STEINBRECHER
TO HIS FAMILY,

Somme River, France, August 12, 1916,

World War I

T
he 1916 English and French offensive against German positions in the Somme River region was designed to destroy the
front that had existed since Germany invaded France in 1914.
The attack commenced with a ferocious eight-day bombardment
against the German troops from 1,500 guns, one positioned every
20 yards along the Allied line. On the morning of July 1, 1916, the
English and French troops advanced against entrenched German
positions on higher ground. Because the British infantry, known as
"Tommys," had been drilled to march slowly and in alignment, they
were mowed down by German machinegunners. Britain's single
greatest calamity during the war, the engagement left 58,000 killed
or wounded. Fighting continued for months until the worn-out
Allied troops pushed the German line back far enough to force a
retreat. The Somme campaign featured an early use of night attacks
and the first, albeit premature, implementation of tanks. However,
only 9 of the 49 armored vehicles made it through the battle. In all,
the British incurred 420,000 casualties, the French 200,000, and
the Germans 500,000. Friedrich Steinbrecher, a soldier in Kaiser

Wilhelm II's army, offers a German infantryman's point of view of the conflict.

> *I want to keep running on—to stand still and look is horrible. "A wall of dead and wounded!" How often have I read the phrase! Now I know what it means.*

Somme.

The whole history of the world cannot contain a more ghastly word! All the things I am now once more enjoying—bed, coffee, rest at night, water—seem unnatural and as if I had no right to them. And yet I was only there a week.

At the beginning of the month we left our old position. During the lorry and train journey we were still quite cheery. We knew what we were wanted for. Then came bivouacs, an "alarm", and we were rushed up through shell-shattered villages and barrage into the turmoil of war. The enemy was firing with 12-inch guns. There was a perfect torrent of shells. Sooner than we expected we were in the thick of it. First in the artillery position. Columns were tearing hither and thither as if possessed. The gunners could no longer see and hear . . . and there was a deafening noise: the cries of wounded, orders, reports.

At noon the gunfire became even more intense, and then came the order: "The French have broken through. Counter-attack!"

We advanced through the shattered wood in a hail of shells. I don't know how I found the right way. Then across an expanse of shell craters, on and on. Falling down and getting up again. Machine guns were firing. I had to cut across our own barrage and the enemy's. I am untouched.

At last we reach the front line. Frenchmen are forcing their way in. The tide of battle ebbs and flows. Then things get quieter. We have not fallen back a foot. Now one's eyes begin to see things. I want to keep running on—to stand still and look is horrible. "A wall of dead and wounded!" How often have I read the phrase! Now I know what it means.

I have witnessed scenes of heroism and of weakness. Men who can endure every privation. Being brave is not only a matter of will, it also requires strong nerves, though the will can do a great deal. A Divisional Commander dubbed us the "Iron Brigade" and said he had never seen anything like it. I wish it had all been only a dream, a bad dream. And yet it was a joy to see such heroes stand and fall. The bloody work cost us 177 men. We shall never forget Chaulmes and Vermandovillers.

Steinbrecher was killed in action in 1917. Outside the town of Vermandovillers, France, is a German cemetery containing the graves of 9,455 individual soldiers—alongside a mass grave of 13,200.

Daily Life

Dead soldiers on the field at Gettysburg

PRIVATE JOHN C. DAVIS
TO HIS PARENTS,

Pennsylvania, July 2, 1863,

Civil War

J im Davis, a small-town blacksmith from Massachusetts, had four boys enlist in the Union army. His eldest son died in the notorious Andersonville prison, and two others were wounded at Antietam. His youngest son, John, wrote the following letter.

Dear Father and Mother:

We are somewhere in Pennsylvania and there's a big battle going on as all day the cannons have been sounding like thunder in the distance. Jim, my bunkie, says it won't be bad and not to be scared, but I am. Most of the men are writing home as we are to march all night to get into position in the morning. I've got so much to write I don't know where to begin. When I reached the Battery the sergeant asked me if I could ride and I said, "Yes, sir." So now I'm the lead rider of number one gun. I have to take care of my two horses and harness. They are a good pair and the work isn't so hard. First few days there was a lot of drilling and then orders came to move out. Jim Haley, my bunkie, rides the pole horses and has been in the army over a year. He's a year older than me and we get along fine. Food isn't much like home but I'm so hungry I can eat anything any time. Even hardtack tastes good soaked in grease and fried. Gee, Ma, I'd give a lot for one of your apple pies. First night we camped on a big farm and orders were to take only the top rail from the fences for fire. The fences didn't last long because the second rail was the top one after the first was gone. The farmer was mad as blazes but Jim said it served him right as he acted like Johnny Reb. Next day was awful hot and dusty. Folks along the road gave us water and we drank quarts, so now half the battery are sick. One place where we stopped to eat a farmer drove up with a barrel of cider in a farm cart. He asked five cents a glass, money in advance. Nobody had any money because pay day is a long way off, so Jim got some of the boys to sass the farmer and keep him busy while he got a long auger from the tool cart and bored a hole right through the bottom of the wagon and cider barrel. Horse pails from the battery came in handy to catch the cider. Tasted mighty good and everybody was happy except the farmer when he tried to draw a glass for an officer. When he found out why the barrel was dry he said it was a d—n smart Yankee trick and drove off. No fun to march all day in the rain, roads all mud and full of ruts. The horses get tired, the guns get stuck and everybody pushes and pries with rails; it's slow travel and dirty work. Been awful hot today and everybody is dead tired but the orders are forward toward those noisy cannon. I can't tell you how funny I feel knowing tomorrow I'll see a big battle. Kind of scared inside but I'm not going to run. There goes the bugle so good-bye. Write me, care of the battery. The sergeant said I'll get it sometime.

Your son,

John

I can't tell you how funny I feel knowing tomorrow I'll see a big battle. Kind of scared inside but I'm not going to run. There goes the bugle so good-bye.

On July 7, 1863, Jim Davis received the following note from a sergeant in the Massachusetts light artillery: "I am sorry to report that your son was instantly killed as the battery went into action on July 3. He was a brave young soldier and acted like a veteran under fire. He was buried on the hillside near the battery position." John had died at Gettysburg, the memorable battle that pitted Confederate general Robert E. Lee's army of 75,000 against the Union general George Meade's 97,000. The fight culminated in Confederate general George E. Pickett's famous charge against Union positions at Cemetery Ridge. Fifty minutes later, the South had suffered 10,000 casualties, with combined battle losses on both sides of 51,000. Together with the Union victory at Vicksburg the next day on July 4, the battle is considered a turning point in the war. John C. Davis, the "brave young soldier," was just 14 years old.

Lenchen allerliebste!

           Two more fine letters came today,
dated June 14 and 18, with all the other recent ones still hardly more
than touched on! How can I possibly hope to catch up with such a grand
correspondent, at any rate before my return to her arms! Writing, as you
know, is something best reserved for evening hours - just as in your own
case. This is true no matter how langorously dull our days may be, which
makes it all the more regrettable. Four hours each evening is the most
I dare count on for everything I'd like to cover - writing, reading,
practicing up at the Conservatory, photographic work at the club, and
perhaps a bit of a snack at the RCC before it closes at 10½ which omits
the occasional movie and talk-fest we're exposed to. For you too, darling,
I know the evenings aren't long, perhaps even less so than mine. Yet
you manage to crowd in ever so much, and that on top of a busy day at the
office and a commuter's trip home! How you do it all is still something
of a mystery despite the recent careful explanation, and I certainly admire you immensely for it!

           It's so good to hear that the parcel sent some two months ago has
reached you safely and in such good condition, darling. It's small wonder that you tossed in bed after examining so closely those remarkable
works of art - they are that, in fact - snuggled in the letter folder!
You can be sure I'll be glad to help clarify the finer points when I'm
back, although it may be somewhat awkward if you insist on having them
explained in the darkroom. However, we've been known to solve such problem
before, haven't we darling? I can hardly wait to try the experiment again!
The red leather portfolio used to enclose not music but Adolf's
papers, orders and suchlike trifles awaiting the all-highest signature.
I hope you're now properly awed and respectful. It came from the Braunes
Haus in Munich, as did the silver and some other souvenirs, so perhaps
we do have something to start our own little museum collection with! In
my next package, darling, there'll be more silver, this from Butcher Heinrich's home, all nicely engraved with SS. You needn't use it if it proves
a revolting thought, but let's keep the damn stuff for a while anyway. It's
legitimate trophies of war, don't you agree? The armbands I shoved in (as
also the compass and pencils) mainly to fill out chinks in the parcel.
The same for the caps. These may all prove pleasant little souvenirs for
friends or their children. Another item in the coming parcel will be a
magnificently illustrated large volume on Da Vinci, something that will

"MISCHA" [LAST NAME UNKNOWN] TO HIS LOVE,

Heidelberg, Germany, June 27, 1945, World War II

This is a most extraordinary letter and one of my favorites. It was written by an obviously well-educated American soldier, possibly an officer, shortly after Germany's surrender in World War II. After the war, Germany was quickly divided into four sectors occupied by France, England, the United States, and Russia—ultimately separating the country into what became known as East and West Germany. As in all wars preceding and following World War II, soldiers from each side, winners and losers, looted whatever they thought would be of commercial value, interest, or practical use. Vast cultural treasures and machinery were systematically removed by the Russian army—many individual GIs helped themselves, too. In this letter, Mischa not only refers to what he has already looted, but unabashedly describes his plans to steal more. The letter fascinates me because despite some clues, I cannot identify Mischa. He is clearly knowledgeable about music; he mentions the highly regarded musicologist Alfred Einstein (Albert's cousin), refers to Köchel's index of Mozart's works, mentions someone with the unusual name of Hugh Nibley (the Mormon scholar?)—yet who is

Mischa? He not only *writes* about looting, the stationery he used bears the blind-stamp impression of the Nazi eagle and swastika, and was *stolen* from the office of the Gauleiter (district leader) of Munich and Upper Bavaria.

Ironically, it was easier to identity the unnamed Gauleiter than the soldier who pilfered his paper. Paul Giesler would have celebrated his fiftieth birthday not two weeks prior to Mischa's letter had he still been alive. Giesler joined the Nazis in 1922, rising through the ranks as district leader for several regions and developing a reputation for using brutal terrorist methods to maintain order. In April 1944, he was appointed Gauleiter for southern Germany after sanctioning the murder of members of the "White Rose," a German resistance group. In his last will, Hitler had even proposed Giesler as Heinrich Himmler's successor. Giesler and his wife died a few days after a poorly executed suicide attempt on May 8, 1945, in Berchtesgaden, while fleeing the U.S. Army. But, if anyone can identify Mischa, please let me know!

Lenchen allerliebste!

Two more fine letters came today, dated June 14 and 18, with all the other recent ones still hardly more than touched on! How can I possibly hope to catch up with such a grand correspondent, at any rate before my return to her arms! Writing, as you know is something best reserved for evening hours—just as in your own case. This is true no matter how langorously dull our days may be, which, makes it all the more regrettable. Four hours each evening is the most I dare count on for everything I'd like to cover—writing, reading, practicing up at the Conservatory, photographic work at the club, and perhaps a bit of a snack at the RCC before it closes at 10; which omits the occasional movie and talk-fest we're exposed to. For you too, darling, I know the evenings aren't long, perhaps even less so than mine. Yet you manage to crowd in ever so much, and that on top of a busy day at the office and a commuter's trip home! How you do it all is still something of a mystery despite the recent careful explanation, and I certainly admire you immensely for it!

It's so good to hearthat the parcel sent some two months ago has reached you safely and in such good condition, darling. It's small wonder that you tossed in bed after examining so closely those remarkable works of art—they are that, in fact—snuggled in the letter folder! You can be sure I'll be glad to help clarify the finer points when I'm back, although it may be somewhat awkward if you insist on having them explained in the darkroom. However, we've been known to solve such problems before, haven't we darling? I can hardly wait to try the experiment again!

The red leather portfolio used to enclose not music but Adolf's papers, orders and suchlike trifles awaiting the all-highest signature. I hope you're now properly awed and respectful. It came from the Braunes Haus in Munich, as did the silver and some other souvenirs, so perhaps we do have something to start our own little museum collection with! In my next package, darling, there'll be more silver, this from Butcher Heinrich's home, all nicely engraved with SS. You needn't use it if it proves a revolting thought, but let's keep the damn stuff for a while anyway. It's legitimate trophies of war, don't you agree? The armbands I shoved in (as also the compass and pencils) mainly to fill out chinks in the parcel. The same for the caps. These may all prove pleasant little souvenirs for friends or their children. Another item in the coming parcel will be a magnificently illustrated large volume on Da Vinci, something that will truly warm the cockles of your heart from the first touch of the binding and sight of the pictures! I'm tempted to steal the priceless Köchel Verzeichnis of Mozart's Works that I found on the shelves here. It's a book that's practically unobtainable anywhere outside *libraries and rare private collections, and would cost at least 50 dollars even if in the market. The only deterrent is the stamp of the library in the flyleaf, and this is counterbalanced by the fact that the whole library was built by Carnegie money and most of its books acquired that way. In a sense (or am I inventing convenient pretexts?) it would be poetic justice to "liberate" it from an atmosphere that degraded so much of truth and beauty. I've had it in my office for weeks now where I can delight my eyes with the listing by themes of everything Mozart wrote, and maybe old Nick will get me down yet! If so, please don't rub it in*

The red leather portfolio used to enclose not music but Adolf's papers, orders and suchlike trifles awaiting the all-highest signature. . . . so perhaps we do have something to start our own little museum collection with!

too hard, will you? There will also be odds and ends again, darling, to fill the parcel, so prepare for another load. You already know the reason why I still have the perfumes and bracelet. The pleasure of giving will be tripled and more when the moment comes!

By chance I was handed today two copies of the Nation and one New Republic, and to my surprise and pleasure there was Haggin's criticism of Einstein's Mozart biography which you had mentioned! You can guess that it was read with all the greater interest. I don't know, of course, that Haggin's excerpts and criticisms are fairly made. Einstein is a very esteemed author and offhand I'd give him the nod in any dispute with a mere scrivener, even if it were a Newman instead of Haggin (whom, as you know, I generally agree with and respect). In any case, darling, we can wait until my return for a decision on this biography. There are enough in our collection (I mean on Mozart alone) to satisfy us on almost every point. And the main thing is to study and play the music, after all!

And so I come to another close, sweetheart. This because there have already been two interruptions to delay things and the evening will be gone with the wind as far as the conservatory is concerned. Hugh Nibley has been sitting here patiently waiting for the Conservatory session, and I think you'll agree that 8.30 isn't too soon to start. Tomorrow will bring another chat, darling, and I hope a longer one. Meanwhile all my fondest love, a world of longing for the big day of reunion (which should with luck be no later than sometime in September) and a million good wishes in every department including the flag-waving! Your hale and hearty but rapidly spreading

Mischa

The enclosed is something you'll have to put beside the pictures with a big sign tacked up reading: "Off Limits to All Unauthorized Personnel. This Means You."

Soldiers in Vietnam preparing for a helicopter pickup at a landing zone

SPECIALIST 4TH CLASS GEORGE OLSEN TO RED,

November 23, 1969,

Vietnam War

During the Vietnam War, the men of the 75th Ranger Regiment fought three years of sustained combat—the longest of any Ranger unit in its 300-year history. Two members of Olsen's unit, Company G, attached to the 23rd Infantry (Americal Division), were awarded the Medal of Honor. The company's military record during the war was impressive: It participated in 662 combat missions and defended Firebase Fat City, LZ Baldy, and Chu Lai. Olsen was killed in action on March 3, 1970, at the age of 23.

Red,

We've been going pretty strong over here lately, and we're starting to pay the price. We lost a man on one of our teams operating out of Duc Pho two days ago when he pulled a one-man assault on a line of NVA [North Vietnamese Army] who had half his team pinned down. He beat off the NVA but was killed doing it, and has been nominated for the CMH [Congressional Medal of Honor], which along with the

Purple Heart is one medal I've no use for. We went out on one mission up here which made the papers, even if they didn't get the whole story right. We knocked [off] two base camps, killed one NVA, who could've been taken prisoner if our ARVNs [Army of the Republic of Vietnam— Vietnam] hadn't cut him down out of hate and general principle, and took one VC [Vietcong] prisoner.

One hold opened up less than 50 meters away, and I watched its occupant shoulder an AK [and] point it right at me. . . . How he ever missed . . . me . . . at that range I'll never know, . . .

It was a real textbook operation, but the one we went on yesterday turned out to be the shortest on record and was almost Charlie's big inning. We were to have been inserted with another team for a one-day operation against an arms repair factory with an estimated battalion camped in the general area. I think that estimate too conservative. We went in with two choppers, a chase ship and two [gunships]. When we were about 10 feet off the LZ and our interpreter and I were halfway out on the landing skid, about two seconds from the ground, the feces really hit the fan. On the other chopper the man on the skid was about to jump [to the ground] when a .30-cal machine gun opened up directly under him—he had jumped almost onto [an enemy] bunker. The pilot

*saw another bunker directly in front of him, and the woodline for 360°
was a string of blinking tree lights. What I could personally see out of
my door were spider holes opening up and green tracers coming in. One
hold opened up less than 50 meters away, and I watched its occupant
shoulder an AK [and] point it right at me. Then all I could see was
muzzle flashes, and we had our own little duel right there as he tried
for me and I did my best to walk my tracers up on him and hose him
out of existence. How he ever missed not only me but a target the size
of a Huey at that range I'll never know, but I can see that rifle winking at me. Just as my tracers got up to him I ran out of ammo, which is
about the most frustrating thing that's happened to me yet.*

*The whole thing was morbidly fascinating, and during the whole
exchange I was never scared, which scares me now. I think the whole
thing was that for once you could actually see your enemy, which doesn't
happen too often in war, and the only thought in my mind was to nail
him before he nailed me. There was simply no room for fear. We came
back with one chopper losing fuel and oil, with an underbelly in pieces
but—miraculously—no one was hurt. The Cobras who worked the
area over as we left took fire from .51 cal MGs [machine guns], yet the
major who asked for the operation insisted we still go in—11 men to
assault a battalion!! If I get the opportunity, I'll tell you honestly that I
will kill that son-of-a-bitch. I have more hatred and contempt for him
than I ever thought I could possibly feel for any human being. If there's
one thing I can't abide, it's an armchair leader who sends his men off to
die on hopeless, meaningless operations. To be killed is one thing, to die
senselessly is another. The major piloting the lead ship refused to reinsert
us and put us all in for air medals with "V" for valor for the way we
helped out his door gunners in their hour of need. I'd put him in for
sainthood for having the guts to tell his superior to go to hell, that he
didn't want 11 men on his conscience, and under no circumstance was
he going to put us on the ground. I would definitely give credit for all
of us coming out of that in one piece to Almighty God. We definitely*

had an extra, unseen passenger riding with us that day. If they had opened up 10 seconds later, we'd all still be out there. It's as close as I've ever been yet to hell, and I hope it's as close as I'll ever be.

George

GENERAL GEORGE WASHINGTON TO THE CONTINENTAL CONGRESS,

Valley Forge, New Jersey, December 23, 1777,

Revolutionary War

Although the autumn of 1777 brought General George Washington the welcome news that British general John Burgoyne had surrendered nearly 6,000 troops at Saratoga, he also discovered that Samuel Adams and several New England leaders had formed the "Conway Cabal," an effort to replace him as commander in chief. Reflecting on his own reluctance to accept leadership of the revolutionary forces, Washington had previously written his wife, Martha, in 1775: "You may believe me . . . that, so far from seeking this appointment, I have used every endeavor in my power to avoid it." Though not exposed to the harshest winter of the American Revolutionary War, the soldiers who reached camp at Valley Forge were a worn-out, indifferent lot. A serious shortage of supplies had considerably damaged the men's morale, leading Gouverneur Morris, then part of a commission sent to report on conditions at the camp, to observe: "An Army of skeletons appeared before our eyes, naked, starved, sick, discouraged." But a surgeon from Connecticut noted, "With what cheerfulness he meets his foes and encounters every hardship—if barefoot—he labours through the mud and cold with a song in his mouth extolling war and Washington—if his food be bad—he eats it notwithstanding with seeming content, blesses God for a good stomach, and whistles it into indigestion." The following letter was Washington's response to critics in the Continental Congress.

★

Sir:

Full as I was in my representation of matters in the Commys. departmt. yesterday, fresh, and more powerful reasons oblige me to add, that I am now convinced, beyond a doubt that unless some great and capital change suddenly takes place in that line, this Army must inevitably be reduced to one or other of these three things. Starve, dissolve, or disperse, in order to obtain subsistence in the best manner they can; rest assured Sir this is not an exaggerated picture, but that I have abundant reason to support what I say.

Yesterday afternoon receiving information that the Enemy, in force, had left the City, and were advancing towards Derby with apparent design to forage, and draw Subsistance from that part of the Country, I order'd the Troops to be in readiness, that I might give every opposition in my power; when, behold! to my great mortification, I was not only informed, but convinced, that the Men were unable to stir on Acct. of Provision, and that a dangerous Mutiny begun the Night before, and with difficulty was suppressed by the spirited exertion's of some officers was still much to be apprehended on acct. of their want of this Article. . . .

All I could do under these circumstances was, to send out a few light Parties to watch and harrass the Enemy, whilst other Parties were instantly detached different ways to collect, if possible, as much Provision as would satisfy the present pressing wants of the Soldiery. But will this answer? No Sir: three or four days bad weather would prove

The Prayer at Valley Forge by H. Bruckner

our destruction. What then is to become of the Army this Winter? and if we are as often without Provisions now, as with it, what is to become of us in the Spring, when our force will be collected, with the aid perhaps of Militia, to take advantage of an early Campaign before the Enemy can be reinforced? These are considerations of great magnitude, meriting the closest attention, and will, when my own reputation is so intimately connected, and to be affected by the event, justify my saying that the present Commissaries are by no means equal to the execution or that the disaffection of the People is past all belief. The misfortune however does in my opinion, proceed from both causes, and tho' I have been tender heretofore of giving any opinion, or lodging complaints, as the change in that departmt. took place contrary to my judgment, and the consequences thereof were predicted; yet, finding that the inactivity of the Army, whether for want of provisions, Cloaths, or other essentials, is charged to my Acct., not only by the common vulgar, but those in power, it is time to speak plain in exculpation of myself; with truth then I can declare that, no Man, in my opinion, ever had his measures more impeded than I have, by every department of the Army. Since the Month of July, we have had no assistance from the Quarter Master Genl . . . to this I am to add, that notwithstanding it is a standing order (and often repeated) that the Troops shall always have two days Provisions by them, that they may be ready at any sudden call, yet, no opportunity has scarce ever yet happened of taking advantage of the Enemy that has not been either totally obstructed or greatly impeded on this Acct., and this tho' the great and crying evil is not all. Soap, Vinegar and other Articles allowed by Congress we see none of nor have seen I believe since the battle of Brandywine; the first indeed we have now little occasion of few men having more than one Shirt, many only the Moiety of one, and Some none at all; in addition to which as a proof of the little benefit received from a Cloathier Genl., and at the same time as a further proof of the inability of an Army under the circumstances of this, to perform the common duties of Soldiers (besides a number of Men confind to Hospitals for want of Shoes, and others in farmers Houses on the same Acct.) we have, by a field return this day made no less than 2898 Men now in Camp unfit for duty because they are bare foot and otherwise naked and by the same return it appears that our whole strength in continental Troops (Including the Eastern Brigades which have joined us since the surrender of Genl. Burgoyne) exclusive of the Maryland Troops sent to Wilmington amount to no more than 8200 in Camp fit for duty. Notwithstanding which, and that, since the 4th Inst. our Numbers fit for duty from the hardships and exposures they have undergone, particularly on Acct. of Blankets (numbers being obliged and do set up all Night by fires, instead of taking comfortable rest in a natural way) have decreased near 2000 Men. We find Gentlemen without knowing whether the Army was really going into Winter Quarters or not (for I am sure no resolution of mine would warrant the remonstrance) reprobating the measure as much as if they thought Men were made of Stocks or Stones and equally insensible of frost and Snow and moreover, as if they conceived it practicable for an inferior Army under the disadvantages I have describ'd our's to be wch. is by no means exagerated to confine a superior one (in all respects well appointed, and provided for a Winters Campaign) within the City of Phila., and cover from depredation and waste the States of Pensa., Jersey, &ca. But what makes this matter still more extraordinary in my eye is, that these very Gentn. who were well apprized of the nakedness of the Troops, from occular demonstration thought their own Soldiers worse clad than others, and advised me, near a Month ago, to postpone the execution of a Plan, I was about to adopt (in consequence of a resolve of Congress) for seizing Cloaths, under strong assurances that an ample supply would be collected in ten days agreeably to a decree of the State not one Article of wch., by the bye, is yet come to hand, should think a Winters Campaign and the covering these States from the Invasion of an Enemy so easy a business. I can assure those Gentlemen that it is a much easier and less distressing thing to draw remonstrances in a comfortable room by a good fire side than to occupy a cold bleak hill and sleep under frost and Snow without Cloaths or Blankets; however, although they seem to have little feeling for the naked, and distressed Soldier, I feel superabundantly for them, and from my Soul pity those miseries, wch. it is neither in my power to relieve or prevent.

It is for these reasons therefore I have dwelt upon the Subject, and it adds not a little to my other difficulties, and distress, to find that much more is expected of me than is possible to be performed, and that upon the ground of safety and policy, I am obliged to conceal the true State of the Army from Public view and thereby expose myself to detraction and Calumny . . .

I much doubt the practicability of holding the Army together much longer. In this I shall, probably, be thought more sincere, when I freely declare that I do not, myself, expect to derive the smallest benefit from any establishment that Congress may adopt, otherwise than as a Member of the Community at large in the good which I am persuaded will result from the measure by making better Officers and better

Troops, and Secondly to point out the necessity of making the Appointments, arrangements, &ca. without loss of time. We have not more than 3 Months to prepare a great deal of business in; if we let these slip, or waste, we shall be labouring under the same difficulties all next Campaign as we have done this, to rectifie mistakes and bring things to order. Military arrangements and movements in consequence, like the Mechanism of a Clock, will be imperfect, and disorderd, by the want of a part; in a very sensible degree have I experienced this in the course of the last Summer, Several Brigades having no Brigadiers appointed to them till late and some not at all; by which means it follows that an additional weight is thrown upon the Shoulders of the Commander in chief to withdraw his attention from the great line of his duty . . . in short there is as much to be done in preparing for a Campaign as in the active part of it; . . .every thing depends upon the preparation that is made in the several departments in the course of this Winter and the success, or misfortunes of next Campaign will more than probably originate with our activity, or supineness this Winter. I am &ca.

G. Washington

With the arrival at Valley Forge on February 23, 1778, of the newly appointed inspector general, Baron von Steuben, the situation improved. Von Steuben's skills in military training had an instant affect upon the troops. When he broke camp in early spring, General Washington took command of an organized and well-disciplined army.

"MADEMOISELLE MISS" TO HER FAMILY,

France, November 18, 1915,

World War I

The following letter is a window into a remarkable, yet today little-known, chapter in America's involvement in World War I. Though the United States did not officially enter the war on the side of the Allies until 1917, during the three years of America's neutrality, thousands of Americans willingly made the hazardous voyage across the Atlantic Ocean to volunteer their services. Though most joined the Allied forces, both sides benefited from the help. The bulk of these American volunteers were women, more than 25,000, ranging in age from 21 to 60. They were a diverse group, but united in a desire to succor the thousands upon thousands of wounded and destitute soldiers and civilians who desperately needed care and assistance. For the most part, these women served in a variety of medical capacities, usually in the military or as a member of a relief organization such as the Salvation Army or the Red Cross. The letters that many of these women wrote back to their loved ones were often used to solicit additional humanitarian aid for use in the countries overwhelmed by the catastrophe that had been unleashed.

"Mademoiselle Miss," as the soldiers she nursed called her, was one such American volunteer. The daughter of an ex-medical director of the U.S. Navy, she was in France at the outbreak of the war. Initially, she served as a helper, then, learning "that an examination was to be held for a nurse's diploma in the French Red Cross, she studied day and night, faced nine doctors in an oral examination of two and a half hours, and passed with credit." Her diploma was signed by the minister of war. Commissioned a lieutenant, she served in a French military hospital near the Marne River during some of the most grueling battles of the war.

Her letters, written "for one and for one only," were collected into a slender volume published in 1916. In keeping with the spirit of the time, in order to protect her real identity from unladylike publicity, her nom de guerre also became her nom de plume. Published without her knowledge and titled *Mademoiselle Miss,* the collection was "justified only in the hope that they may reach a wider circle and bring help to the heroic France." The book subsequently went through six printings. To this day, Mademoiselle Miss's real identity remains unknown.

Night before last I believe I saved a man for good, who would not have survived the night. But oh, what I need is a great strong intelligent man, always devoted and always right there to follow instructions. He should be six feet, never tired, never out of humor, tender as a woman, and muscled like Ajax! What a lot we could do!

I have tried to hint my gratitude for the generous gifts coming to this poverty-stricken hospital. The goods will be no idle superfluity, I can tell you. Up to now we have been allowed almost nothing to work with, and now a general order has gone forth from the Army Headquarters to economize on that. When I tell you that I have one large needle for my whole Pavilion, and that I am obliged to give on an average of fifteen injections a day with it and as if that were not enough, the doctor frequently asks to borrow it for another hospital, you may guess how it all goes. But when the doctor brings it back he knows I hate to lend it he always says with his most winning smile "I am bringing back the baby to his mother."

No child ever awaited Santa Claus with half the impatience that seizes me every time I think of the arrival of the Rochambeau. [Steamship sent to France from America with hospital supplies.] I feel more like Cherry-Garrard and his comrades, shut up in their Antarctic hole for the winter, wondering how long supplies will hold out, and when the ship will come. Really, it is poverty beyond description, only the strange part of it is that you would never suspect anything of the sort if you should enter the gates of our little Hospital on a sunny morning when flags are flying and fir trees, carefully planted as if it were a terrace at Versailles, throw their pointed shadows across the frosted paths care-free as you please. Ah, it is what makes the charm of the boulevards and the tragedy of the Parisian garrets.

The father of one of my wounded, a rich merchant of Havre, has given me two thermometers one that descends automatically and I love it; but oh, the lacks! Perhaps the hardest to bear, now that I have provided myself with instruments and the Rochambeau has sailed, are the alimentary and medicinal ones.

One man I am keeping alive on malted milk ordered from Paris and fresh eggs the hospital milk being utterly undrinkable, and the eggs preserved. The Head Surgeon regards my little efforts as a symptom of benign lunacy, but he lets me do as I please. Alas, sentiment, intuition, endeavor, don't take the place of science. When I realize my actual ignorance it would utterly terrify me if I did not know I am meant to be just here, and am learning every day from experience, if not from books and masters.

You can't imagine, I suppose, that we laugh and jest all day long? Yet so it is, and if you can't do that, you might as well get out, for all the good you will ever do a French *wounded soldier. Why, I believe his very wounds wouldn't heal if he were not allowed to make merry over them, and he will jest with you up to the hour before he dies a mixture of wit and pathos too poignant ever to reproduce.*

Number nine, contusion cerebral trepannation, etc., has just waked up. He sees me writing. "Mademoiselle, will you give my greetings to your family?" ("Mademoiselle, donnez bien le bonjour à votre famille pour moi, n'est-ce pas?") *Echoed by No. 4. "And mine also, Mademoiselle."* ("Ainsi que moi, Mademoiselle.") *Poor fellow, he can hardly be here long!*

My little boy from Havre, 19 years old, with resection of the shoulder and a temperature that refuses to moderate (which disquiets me much, for there is no obvious reason save a high-strung temperament), speaks English very well. One day he was looking at my insignia A. D. F. and a bar. "What's your rank, Mademoiselle?" I told him. "Then I think they should call you Lieutenant of the Life Guards!" Pretty, wasn't it? I suppose that you know that war surgery calls for antiseptics much more powerful than are used in ordinary peace operations. For instance, alcohol 95%. It is no joke to pour alcohol into a gaping wound, and No. 1, though brave as can be, resents it intensely. One day, as he gripped the sides of the operating table to keep from upsetting my arrangements, he gave me a quizzical look: "Sister, why are you tempting me so when you know very well that the government has strictly forbidden our taking any sort of alcohol?"

I wish you could see my ward just now, with the wintry sunlight streaming in, making us all think we are warmer! Imagine, it is not yet December, and the mercury is down nearly to zero Fahrenheit. It takes some nerve to dress in white linen with sleeves above the elbows! But we don't mind when the sun shines, making bright gold patches everywhere, and striking through the trophy of flags that I have arranged down there at the end of the ward to the great delight of the children.

There hang the flags of all the Allies, except Japan, which wasn't to be had, and there is a wee Stars and Stripes at the point of the shield made by our obliging carpenter. The electric lights overhead are draped in tricolor, and on the table is one red rose brought me from Paris.

It is not so bad for a "front" hospital, and wonder of wonders, it's clean *and that by dint of much strategy. It used to be awful. But there are two ways of appealing to a Frenchman, through his heart and through his pride. When you work both together, you have his body and soul. And so, when my orderlies saw me on my knees scrubbing, they came to the rescue, and then I clinched the matter with the flags and the suggestion that* ours *should be the model ward. It worked! But of course one doesn't count on the morrow.*

THEODORE ROOSEVELT TO HENRY CABOT LODGE,

on board U.S. transport Yucatan, Tampa,
June 12, 1898, Spanish-American War

Theodore Roosevelt served his country not only as a president of the United States, but also as a soldier, a statesman, a reformer, a prolific author, a cowboy, a rancher, an environmentalist, and a Nobel Prize winner for his efforts as president to end the Russo-Japanese War. Appointed assistant secretary of the Navy by President McKinley, it was "T.R.," as he was known, who boldly instructed Commodore George Dewey to assemble the Asiatic squadron at Hong Kong in case of war with Spain. His intention to block the Spanish fleet's departure was militarily brilliant but politically unwise; he had overstepped his authority by issuing the order during Secretary of Navy Long's absence. Dewey's subsequent and decisive victory at Manila on May 1, 1898, however, led T.R.'s superiors to overlook the impropriety of his actions. Commissioned as a lieutenant colonel in the 1st Volunteer Cavalry Regiment (which the press nicknamed the Rough Riders), Roosevelt drew on cowboys, Native Americans, Texas Rangers, lumberjacks, and some of his Harvard friends to constitute his unit. They sailed from Tampa the day after T.R. wrote this letter to his good friend Henry Cabot

Lodge, coauthor of *Hero Tales from American History* and a future senator from Massachusetts. The Rough Riders landed in Cuba on June 22 and saw action two days later.

Dear Cabot:

I wonder if it would be possible for you to tell the Administration, that is, the President, and if necessary the Secretary of War, just what is going on here and the damage that is being done. Of course, I cannot speak publicly in any way; I should be court-martialed if I did, but this letter I shall show to Wood, my Colonel, and it is written after consultation with Gen. Young, my brigade commander. I shall not show this first paragraph to Wood or to Young, for I want to say that it would be impossible to get a better man for Colonel than Wood has shown himself to be, and so far as I am concerned I am entirely content with Young as a Brigade General, but otherwise the mismanagement here is frightful. Wood thinks that if Miles could be given absolute control he would straighten things out and I most earnestly wish the experiment could be tried, though personally I cannot help feeling that Miles might have remedied a great deal that has gone wrong if only he had chosen or had known how. Think of embarking troops by sending their regiments higgledly-piggledly from their camp to the port ten miles away on a one-line railroad without ever assigning to each regiment its transport and without having a single officer detailed to meet the regiment and show them where to go or what they were to do. Our experience was that of every other regiment. We were up the entire night standing by the railway track at Tampa, hoping for trains that did not come. At dawn we were shifted to another railway track, and then owing to some energetic work of Wood and myself succeeded in getting the troops on empty coal cars, in which we came down to the wharf. At the wharf we could find no human being who could tell us what our transport was. Gen. Miles and Gen. Shafter both told us that if we did not find out soon we would not be able to go, and said they knew nothing more about it. The Quartermaster General and the Commissary General were allotting the boats. Neither had an office nor any place where he was to be found. The wharf was over a mile long, jammed with trains, with boats everywhere alongside, ten thousand troops embarking. Through this crowd Wood and I had to hunt until almost at the same time we both found the Quartermaster General. He allotted us a transport and advised us to seize her instantly if we hoped to keep her. The advice was good, for it proved she had been allotted to another regiment—the 71st N.Y. While Wood went out into the stream in a boat which he had seized for the purpose and got aboard the transport and brought her in, I brought up my four hundred men at a double and took possession in the very nick of tine to head off the 71st regiment, which was also advancing for the purpose. Meanwhile they unloaded our stores about a mile off and we had to bring them up by hand. However, all this we could stand, but just as soon as we were all loaded and ready work came that there had been a complete change of plans and that the expedition was indefinitely postponed. As it had taken three days to load all the troops and would take six to unload them and load them again, it was obviously unwise to do anything but keep them on board until there was definite information from Washington. So, thanks to this vacillation of purpose at Washington this is the fifth day we have spent (and the eighth day some of the troops have spent) packed and sweltering on these troop ships in Tampa bay under the semi-tropical June sun. In spite of the sharks, we let the men bathe morning and evening, as it is too hot during the rest of the day. The shore is mere sand, but fortunately we have been moved out of the fetid ditch beside the wharf where we first lay, so that the men can be very rarely sent ashore. We have given them the entire deck and they are packed so close that they can get no exercise and no drill, while the officers, except when inspecting the ship or attending a disembarkation, have to keep to their own cabins.

Now, if this were necessary no one would complain for a moment,

Colonel Roosevelt and his Rough Riders atop the hill they captured in the Battle of San Juan

and the men are perfectly cheerful as it is; but it is absolutely unnecessary; the five days' great heat and crowded confinement are telling visibly upon the spirits and health of the troops. It seems incredible that a place like Tampa should have been chosen without previous inspection, that no improvements should have been made in the railroad facilities at the place during the last month and that the Ordinance and Quartermaster Departments should have fallen into such inextricable confusion; a confusion partly due to their own dilatory inefficiency and partly due to the utter incompetence of the railway managers here and the inadequacy of their system. Finally, it was inexcusable to get the troops to Tampa unless it was intended to embark them, while it seems literally incredible that they could have been embarked before it was intended to use them.

All this is in the past now, but at least it may be possible to prevent such blunders in the future. It should be well determined in advance, before sending troops, that they are to sail, and when they are once sent aboard they should sail forthwith. Agents of the Government, men of push and intelligence, and above all men of youth, should be sent to every point of debarkation to tell exactly the difficulties and the needs and how they can be met. It, of course, goes without saying, that men should be appointed as Generals of Divisions and Brigades who are physically fit, as well as morally and mentally. The Ordnance Dept. in particular needs a thorough shaking up; and there should in every port like this be one responsible head who would be held to a rigid account-ability. Some of the regular army officers were saying today that every day we had remained on these transports had reduced the efficiency of the force just about five percent, while to disembark the men now would mean a serious harm to the morale. They will get over it, of course, just as they would get over the effects of a repulse by the Spaniards, but it would be about as serious as a repulse.

I did not feel that I was fit to be Colonel of this regiment and I was certainly much less fit than Wood, who has done better with it than I pos-sibly could have done, but I am more fit to command a Brigade or a Division or attend to this whole matter of embarking and sending the army than many of those whose business it is to do the work. I do not know whether the circumstances at Tampa were exceptional; if not, there is need of an immediate and radical change or the inefficiency of our Government in 1812 will be more than paralleled.

Naturally this is not a letter that can be shown to anyone, but I am going to keep you informed as to the facts, and for the credit of the coun-try and administration I wish you would try to straighten things out. I know what a fight you have on strictly the line of your own duties, old man, and of course you must not neglect that, no matter what happens to the Administration. You must get Manila and Hawaii; you must prevent any talk of peace until we get Porto Rico and the Philippines as well as secure the independence of Cuba. These jobs are big enough, but if besides doing them you can make the Administration realize that we have to go into this thing with a good heart and have to put the best men into the important positions and insist upon efficiency as the one vital requisite, you will add enormously to the debt the country already owes you.

I see Bronson and my old aid Sharp both got into the fight at Santiago. Lucky fellows! Harry and I are left, so far, but I do most sincerely hope we shall yet be able to get in. We are already in the yellow fever zone and at the beginning of the yellow fever season, and I only hope that no weakness or vacillation will prevent our being put where we can do some service inasmuch as we are already running the risk. I doubt if Cuba is much more unhealthy than the low coast of Florida now.

Give my love to Nannie.

Faithfully yours

The Rough Riders, together with Colonel (later General) "Black Jack" Pershing's African American 10th Cavalry, took Kettle Hill on July 1. Joining yet another all-black outfit, the 24th Infantry, T.R. led the charge up what is known as San Juan Hill— an event that propelled Roosevelt into national prominence. In the engagement, T.R. lost about 90 of his men, nearly 20 percent of the so-called buffalo soldiers, and 50 percent of the officers from the 9th and 10th Cavalry. Roosevelt's outspokenness was characteristic of the man. Another letter published early the following month, describing the horrendous conditions soldiers experienced while awaiting evacuation due to ongoing military incompetence, contributed to the Army's ordering the removal of U.S. troops from Santiago. Yet Secretary of the Army Russell Alger and other generals were furious at Roosevelt and saw to it that he would be denied the Medal of Honor for his valorous charge up San Juan Hill. On January 16, 2001, President Bill Clinton awarded a posthumous medal to Theodore Roosevelt—the only American president ever to receive the nation's highest military decoration.

PRIVATE 1ST CLASS DAVID BOWMAN WRITING HOME,

September 1968,

Vietnam War

David Bowman was an infantryman with Company B, 1st Battalion, 8th Cavalry Regiment, 1st Cavalry Division (Airmobile), the highest-decorated unit in the Vietnam War. Known as the Jumping Mustangs, the 8th Cavalry regiment was based at An Khe and Phong Dien, and received two Presidential Unit Citations as well as the Valorous Unit Citation. Two of the cavalry's four Medal of Honor winners were from Company B. Bowman served from September 1967 through September 1968, and is a retired police inspector, as well as his regiment's historian.

Dear Civilians, Friends, Draft Dodgers, etc.

In the very near future, the undersigned will once more be in your midst, dehydrated and demoralized, to take his place again as a human being with the well-known forms of freedom and justice for all; engage in life, liberty and the somewhat delayed pursuit of happiness. In making your joyous preparations to welcome him back into organized society you might take certain steps to make allowances for the past twelve months. In other words, he might be a little Asiatic from Vietnamesitis and Overseasitis, and should be handled with care. Don't be alarmed if he is infected with all forms of rare tropical diseases. A little time in the "Land of the Big PX" will cure his malady.

Therefore, show no alarm if he insists on carrying a weapon to the dinner table, looks around for his steel pot when offered a chair, or wakes you up in the middle of the night for guard duty. Keep cool when he pours gravy on his dessert at dinner of mixed peaches and Seagrams VO. Pretend not to notice if he acts dazed, eats with his fingers instead of silverware and prefers C-rations to steak. Take it with a smile when he insists on digging up the garden to fill sandbags for the bunker he is building. Be tolerant when he takes his blanket and sheet off the bed and puts them on the floor to sleep on.

Abstain from saying anything about powdered eggs, dehydrated potatoes, fried rice, fresh milk or ice cream. Do not be alarmed if he should jump up from the dinner table and rush to the garbage can to wash his dish with a toilet brush. After all, this has been his standard. Also, if it should start raining, pay no attention to him if he pulls off his clothes, grabs a bar of soap and a towel and runs outdoors for a shower.

When in his daily conversation he utters such things as "Xin loi" and "Choi oi" just be patient, and simply leave quickly and calmly if by some chance he utters "didi" with an irritated look on his face because it means no less than "Get the h— out of here." Do not let it shake you up if he picks up the phone and yells "Sky King forward, Sir" or says "Roger out" for good-by or simply shouts "Working."

Never ask why the Jones' son held a higher rank than he did, and by no means mention the word "extend." Pretend not to notice if at a restaurant he calls the waitress "Numbuh 1 girl" and uses his hat as an ashtray. He will probably be listening for "Homeward Bound" to sound off over AFRS. If he does, comfort him, for he is still reminiscing. Be especially watchful when he is in the presence of women—especially a beautiful woman.

Above all, keep in mind that beneath that tanned and rugged exterior there is a heart of gold (the only thing of value he has left). Treat him with kindness, tolerance, and an occasional fifth of good liquor and you will be able to rehabilitate that which was once (and now a hollow shell) the happy-go-lucky guy you once knew and loved.

Last, but not least, send no more mail to the APO, fill the ice box with beer, get the civvies out of mothballs, fill the car with gas, and get the women and children off the streets—BECAUSE THE KID IS COMING HOME!!!!!

Love,
Dave

Famous Moments

John F. Kennedy aboard *PT 109*

LIEUTENANT JOHN F. KENNEDY

Nauru Island, August 2, 1943,
World War II

The most unusual letter in this book has to be the one scratched on a coconut shell by a future president of the United States. If the South Pacific native to whom it had been entrusted had not delivered it, the course of world history may well have been radically altered. In October 1941, 24-year-old John F. Kennedy received his appointment as an ensign in the U.S. Naval Reserve. After several assignments and additional training, Lieutenant Kennedy took command of *PT 109*, part of the 2nd Torpedo Boat Squadron stationed on Tulagi Island in the South Pacific. The unit's objective was to interdict Japanese supply ships supporting enemy garrisons on the island of New Georgia, provide reconnaissance for U.S. forces in the area, and attack Japanese warships whenever possible. While on night patrol on August 1–2, 1943, the Japanese destroyer *Amagiri* rammed *PT 109* and, in less than 10 seconds, sliced it in two. Of the 13 men on board, two were killed and several were wounded. A small island lay three miles to the southeast, and after offering his life jacket to one of his injured shipmates, Kennedy towed the sailor the entire way by grasping the jacket strap between his teeth. Finding no food or water on the island, everyone swam to a neighboring one—Kennedy once again towing his comrade. Later, Kennedy and Ensign George Ross reached Nauru Island and found several natives. Kennedy scratched out the following message on a coconut shell, handed it to one of the men, and said, "Rendova, Rendova!" indicating the location of his home PT base.

★

> *Nauro Isl Commander . . . native knows pos'it . . . he can pilot . . . 11 alive need small boat . . . Kennedy*

The next day, the natives returned with supplies. One of them spoke near-flawless English and handed Kennedy a letter from Lieutenant Arthur Evans, coastwatcher commander from a New Zealand camp. Evans instructed Kennedy to return with the natives and on August 8, PT 157 rescued the remaining survivors. In addition to a Purple Heart, Kennedy received the Navy and Marine Corps Medal with a citation from Admiral Halsey noting his "courage, endurance and excellent leadership in keeping with the highest traditions of the United States Naval Service." Upon Kennedy's election to the presidency, Kohei Hanami, commander of the *Amagiri,* sent him a letter of congratulations, and during his brief term in office, the president had an opportunity to meet his rescuers and members of the Japanese destroyer. The original coconut shell occupied a place of honor on J. F. K.'s White House desk.

The coconut shell

The *Shannon* awaiting the approach of the *Chesapeake*

CAPTAIN PHILIP BOWES VERE BROKE TO CAPTAIN BLADEN,

on board the HMS Shannon, Halifax,

June 6, 1813, War of 1812

The American frigate *Chesapeake*, first launched in 1800, was in serious need of repairs when America's final war with Great Britain, the War of 1812, broke out. Thirty-two-year-old James Lawrence was the *Chesapeake*'s new captain. (Previous commanders included Isaac Hull and Stephen Decatur, famous for his memorable toast: "Our country! In her intercourse with foreign nations may she always be in the right; but our country, right or wrong!") Lying offshore from Boston, the 38-gun frigate HMS *Shannon*, boasting the best-trained crew in the Royal Navy and commanded by Captain Philip Bowes Vere Broke, with more than six years experience aboard his ship, prepared to issue a one-on-one challenge to the *Chesapeake*. Before the message arrived, Captain Lawrence, a less experienced officer commanding an unmotivated crew, sailed out of harbor and promptly lost his ship in a pitched battle. Although Broke was seriously wounded by a cutlass blow to the head, it was Lawrence who died during the engagement. His last immortal words, "Don't give up the ship!" are among the most famous ever uttered during an American battle.

Of the officers who commanded the *Chesapeake,* all but Isaac Hull suffered a premature conclusion to their lives or careers. Even the ship experienced an ignominious fate. After her capture, she served for a brief time in the Royal Navy before being sold for scrap in 1820 for £500; her timbers were used to build houses in Portsmouth, England. An American training ship christened *Chesapeake* was launched in 1899, but in 1905 she underwent a forced name change because of the first *Chesapeake*'s fate and curse. No American warship has carried the name since.

Sir, I have the honour to inform you, that being close in with Boston lighthouse in H.M.S. under my command, on the 1st inst. I had the pleasure of seeing the US frigate Chesapeake *(whom we had long been watching) was coming out of the harbour to engage the* Shannon; *I took a position between Cape Ann and Cape Cod and then hove-to for him to join us. The enemy came down in a very handsome manner, having three American ensigns flying . . . At half past 5 P.M. the enemy hauled up within hail of us on the starboard side, and the battle began, both ships steering full under their topsails; after exchanging between two and three broadsides, the enemy's ship fell on board us, her mizen channels locking in with our fore rigging. I went forward to ascertain her position; and observing the enemy was flinching from their guns, I gave orders to prepare for boarding. Our gallant hands appointed to the service immediately rushed in, under their respective officers, upon the enemy's decks, driving everything before them with irresistible fury. The enemy made a desperate but disorderly resistance. The firing continued at all the gangways, and between the tops, but in two minutes time the enemy were driven sword in hand from every post. The American flag was hauled down and the proud British Union floated triumphant over it. In another minute they ceased firing from below and called*

No expression I can make use of can do justice to the merits of my valiant officers and crew; the calm courage they displayed during the cannonade and the tremendous precision of their fire, could only be equaled by the ardour with which they rushed to the assault.

for quarter. The whole of this service was achieved in 15 minutes from the commencement of the action.

I have to lament the loss of many of my shipmates, but they fell exulting in their conquest. My brave first Lieutenant, Mr Watt, was slain in the moment of victory, in the act of hoisting the British colours; his death is a severe loss to the service. Mr Aldham, the purser, who had spiritedly volunteered the charge of a party of small-arm men, was killed at his post on the gangway . . . My veteran boatswain, Mr Stephens has lost an arm . . . I am happy to say that Mr Samwell, a midshipman of much merit, is the only other officer wounded besides myself, and he not dangerously. Of my gallant seamen and marines, we had 23 slain and 56 wounded. No expression I can make use of can do justice to the merits of my valiant officers and crew; the calm courage they displayed during the cannonade and the tremendous precision of their fire, could only be equaled by the ardour with which they rushed to the assault. I recomend them all warmly to the protection of the Commander in Chief.

Having received a severe sabre wound at the first onset, whilst charging a party of the enemy who had rallied on their forecastle, I was only capable of giving command till assured our conquest was complete; and then directing second Lieutenant Wallis to take charge of Shannon and secure the prisoners, I left the third Lieutenant, Mr Falkiner (who headed the main deck boarders), in charge of the prize. I beg to recommend these officers to the commander in chief's patronage, for the gallantry they displayed during the action and the skill and judgment they evinced in the anxious duties which thereafter devolved upon them . . .

It is utterly impossible to particularize every brilliant deed performed by my officers and men; but I must mention, when the ships' yard-arms were locked together, that Mr Cosnahan, who commanded in our main-top, finding himself screened from the enemy by the foot of the top-sail, laid out along the main-yard-arm to fire upon them, and shot three in that situation. Mr Smith, who commanded in our foretop, stormed the enemy's fore-top from the fore-yard-arm and destroyed all the Americans remaining on it . . .

The loss of the enemy was about 70 killed and 100 wounded. Among the former were her fourth Lieutenant, a Lieutenant of Marines, the Master and many other officers. Capt. Lawrence is since dead of his wounds. The enemy came into action with a complement of 440 men; the Shannon having picked up some recaptured seamen, had 330. The Chesapeake is a fine frigate, and mounts 49 guns, eighteens on her main-deck, two-and-thirties on her quarter deck and forecastle. Both ships came out of the action in the most beautiful order, their rigging appearing as perfect as if they had only being exchanging a salute. I have the honour to be, etc.

(Signed) P.B.V. BROKE
To Captain the Hon. T. Bladen, CAPEL.

The following letter is from Lieutenant George Budd, U.S. Navy, to Secretary of the Navy Board William Jones, recalling this historic encounter from an American viewpoint.

★

Halifax, June 15th 1813

Sir, The unfortunate death of captain James Lawrence, and Lieutenant Augustus C. Ludlow, has rendered it my duty to inform you of the capture of the late United States frigate Chesapeake. *On Tuesday June 1, at 8 A.M. we unmoored ship, and at meridian got under way from President's Roads, with a light wind from the southward and westward, and proceeded on a cruise. A ship was then in sight in the offing, which had the appearance of a ship of war, and which, from information received from pilot-boats and craft, we believed to be the British frigate* Shannon. *We made sail in chase, and cleared the ship for action. At half past 4 P.M. she hove to with her head to the southward and eastward. At 5 P.M. took in the royals and topgallant sails, and at half past 5, hauled the courses up. At 15 minutes before 6 P.M. the action commenced within pistol shot. The first broadside did great execution on both sides, damaged our rigging, killed among others, Mr. White, the sailing master, and wounded Captain Lawrence. In about 12 minutes after the commencement of the action, we fell on board of the enemy, and immediately after, one of our arm chests on the quarterdeck was blown up by a hand-grenade thrown from the enemy's ship. In a few minutes, one of the captain's aids came on the gun-deck to inform me that the boarders were called. I immediately called the boarders away, and proceeded to the spar deck were I found that the enemy had succeeded in boarding us, and gained possession of our quarterdeck. I immediately gave orders to haul on board the fore-tack, for the purpose of shooting the ship clear of the other, and then made an attempt to* regain the quarterdeck, but was wounded and was thrown down on the gun-deck. I again made an effort to collect the boarders, but in the meantime the enemy had gained complete possession of the ship. I there found Captain Lawrence and Lieutenant Ludlow, both mortally wounded; the former had been carried below, previously to the ship's being boarded; the latter was wounded in attempting to repel the boarders. Among those who fell early in the action, was Mr. Edward J. Ballard, the 4th lieutenant, and lieutenant James Broom, of the marines. I herein enclose to you a return of the killed and wounded, by which you will perceive that every officer, upon whom the charge of the ship would devolve, was either killed or wounded, previously to her capture. The enemy reports the loss of Mr. Watt, their first lieutenant, the purser, the captain's clerk, and 23 seamen killed; and Captain Broke, a midshipman and 56 seamen wounded. The Shannon, had, in addition to her full complement, an officer and 16 men belonging to the Belle Poule, and a part of the crew belonging to the Tenedos.

George Budd

GENERAL ROBERT E. LEE
TO THE ARMY OF NORTHERN VIRGINIA,

Headquarters, Army of Northern Virginia,

April 10, 1865, Civil War

G eneral Lee's retreat from Petersburg, Virginia, and the fall of Richmond on April 3, 1865, signaled the Confederacy's collapse; four days later, Union General Ulysses S. Grant sent Lee a message requesting his surrender. On April 9, Lee, after making one last desperate attempt to break through the Union lines blocking his way south, recognized the futility of further military action, and agreed to meet Grant at Appomattox Court House to sign an instrument of surrender. That evening, Lee's military secretary Colonel Charles Marshall sat with Lee and several others. Marshall recalled that "at a fire in front of his tent, and after some conversation about the army and the events of the day in which his feelings toward his men were strongly expressed, he told me to prepare an order to the troops. . . ." Marshall was unable to attend to the order that night. On the following day, Lee, "finding that the order had not been prepared, directed [Marshall] to get into his ambulance, which stood near his tent, and placed an orderly to prevent anyone from approaching us. I made a draft in pencil and took it to General Lee who struck out a paragraph, which he said would tend to keep alive the feeling existing between North and South, and made one or two other changes." Transmittal copies were sent to commanders and other members of Lee's staff; some of these, signed by Lee, are occasionally offered for sale in the autograph market.

After four years of arduous service, marked by unsurpassed courage and fortitude, the Army of Northern Virginia has been compelled to yield to overwhelming numbers and resources. I need not tell the survivors of so many hard-fought battles, who have remained steadfast to the last, that I have consented to this result from no distrust of them; but, feeling that valor and devotion could accomplish nothing that could compensate for the loss that would have attended the continuation of the contest, I have determined to avoid the useless sacrifice of those whose past services have endeared them to their countrymen. By the terms of the agreement, officers and men can return to their homes and remain there until exchanged. You will take with you the satisfaction that proceeds from the consciousness of duty faithfully performed; and I earnestly pray that a merciful God will extend to you His blessing and protection. With an increasing admiration of your constancy and devotion to your country, and a grateful remembrance of your kind and generous consideration of myself, I bid you an affectionate farewell.

R. E. Lee, General

Lee's surrender at Appomattox did not end the Civil War. It was not until April 18 that General Sherman for the North and General Johnston for the South agreed on terms concluding the Carolinas campaign. President Johnson declared the war finally over on May 10, 1865.

BRIGADIER GENERAL ANTHONY McAULIFFE TO THE GERMAN COMMANDER,

Bastogne, Belgium, December 22, 1944,

World War II

During the Allies's attempt to break Nazi strongholds in Germany's Aachen and Saar sectors, they were forced to leave some areas with reduced defenses. It was in one such location, the Ardennes Mountains along the German/Belgian border, that Hitler began his famous counteroffensive to split the Allied invasion and cut off their supply lines. Under a heavy fog on December 16, 1944, the German commander, Field Marshal Gerd von Rundstedt, launched the attack. Two days later, McAuliffe's 101st Airborne Division was ordered in and told to "Hold Bastogne." Almost immediately, McAuliffe's men found themselves surrounded by a superior German force.

At 11:30 A.M. on December 22, four German officers carrying a white flag approached the lines of the 2nd Battalion, 327th Infantry, bearing an ultimatum signed "The German Commander." It read: "The fortune of war is changing. This time the U.S.A. forces in and near Bastogne have been encircled by strong German armored units. More German armored units have crossed the river Ourthe near Ourtheville, have taken Marche and reached St.

Hubert by passing through Hompres-Sibret-Tillet. Libramont is in German hands. There is only one possibility to save the encircled U.S.A. troops from total annihilation: that is honorable surrender of the encircled town. In order to think it over, a term of two hours will be granted beginning with the presentation of this note. If this proposal should be rejected, one German Artillery Corps and six heavy A.A. Battalions are ready to annihilate the U.S.A. Troops in and near Bastogne. The order for firing will be given immediately after this two-hour term. All the serious civilian losses caused by this Artillery fire would not correspond with the well-known American humanity. [Signed] The German Commander." McAuliffe read the letter at division headquarters, shouted "Nuts!" threw the note away, and walked out. Reminded later about the German commander's message, McAuliffe decided to reply. He asked his staff about an appropiate response. They suggested that his first monosyllabic retort would be perfect, so he sent the following.

22 December 1944

To the German Commander:

NUTS!

The American Commander

When the note was handed over to the German officers, they were confused by the general's succinct reply. Colonel Joseph Harper informed them, "If you don't know what 'nuts' means, in plain English it is the same as 'Go to hell.' And let me tell you something else, if you continue to attack we'll kill every goddamned

(Opposite): American troops during the Battle of the Bulge

German that tries to break through our lines." On Christmas Eve, McAuliffe recalled the recent events in a letter to his troops, concluding, "Allied Troops are counterattacking in force. We continue to hold Bastogne. By holding Bastogne, we assure the success of the Allied Armies. We know that our Division Commander, General Taylor, will say: 'Well done!' We are giving our Country and our loved ones at home a worthy Christmas present and being privileged to take part in this gallant feat of arms are truly making for ourselves a Merry Christmas." The 101st held on, and by December 26, tanks from the 4th Armored Division of the U.S. Third Army broke through to relieve the defenders of Bastogne.

Human Cost of War

2ND LIEUTENANT DANIEL HARVEY HILL TO HIS MOTHER,

Comargo, Mexico, August 6, 1846,

Mexican War

Hill served in the 4th U.S. Artillery, fighting in northern Mexico under the command of future president Zachary Taylor. Hill's letter describes the army's unimpeded progress along the Rio Grande. He comments liberally and scornfully about the volunteers in the Mexican War, but in reality these soldiers fought effectively alongside the regular U.S. Army. The Mississippi Rifles, commanded by the future president of the Confederate States of America, Jefferson Davis, had one of the best records at the war's conclusion, and Hill was cited for meritorious conduct in actions at Contreras and Churubusco.

I arrived yesterday where we will probably remain six weeks or two months, when we advance toward Monterey. Burita, Matamoros, Reynosa, Comargo and Mien have all submitted without firing a gun. We have now more than four hundred miles of the enemy's country in our possession, the richest and loveliest country I have ever seen, numbering nearly fifty thousand inhabitants. It is mighty gratifying to me

that all the towns have submitted to the <u>Regulars</u>, the rascally volunteers have only cooperated in the taking of one wretched little village. The volunteers are ready enough to murder, rob, and pillage the wretched inhabitants after they have surrendered. Murder, rape and robbery have

The people are generally as dark as Indians and have the Indian features strongly marked. I have however seen some of them who would pass for Americans. . . .

been committed by those fiends in broad daylight. But to a more agreeable subject, we came up by water and were fine . . . a distance of four hundred miles. The current was so strong that we . . . only ascend with difficulty. When I first saw the Rio Grande at its mouth I thought it little more than a muddy little creek, scarcely larger than Alison's Creek when swollen. But I was more impressed with its beauty & grandeur the longer I was on it. Beautiful prairies of almost boundless extent are seen for many miles above its mouth, the dense chapparal then succeeds, the banks then become higher and are sparsely timbered with muskeet, afterward the oak, ash, elm of huge dimensions line the banks. The River was thickly settled in many places, continuous cornfields extended for miles. Below the Matamoros, the inhabitants had seen volunteers and were dreadfully afraid of troops. These scoundrels had committed all sorts of rascalities among them and had even in very wantoness fired on *them as their boats passed. Above Matamoros, they kept aloof until informed that we were <u>Regulars</u> they then approached us with much confidence. Men, women & children came on board our boat and engaged in traffic with the captain for some cotton fabrics, which he only charged them three pieces for. I went to many of their houses. They are generally made entirely of cane, in some instances crooked sticks were placed upright and thatched over with cane. In front of their huts, they generally had a sort of scaffolding put up and covered over with ears of corn set upright. Under these sheds they spent all their time in good weather. We occasionally saw a house of more pretensions, built of adobes (unburnt brick) but thatched like the rest with cane. The poorer sort of the men were either entirely naked except around the middle or were destitute of shirts and had their pants rolled up as high as possible. The richer class of poor men wear loose trousers and loose shirts open at the collars. The lower class of women have no sleeves to their loose frocks and expose their necks and bosoms. When a stranger approaches, however, they throw the reboso (a sort of shawl) around the head and neck and conceal the defects of their dress. All the <u>male</u> children with few exceptions go entirely naked, but I have not yet seen a naked girl child. The people are generally as dark as Indians and have the Indian features strongly marked. I have however seen some of them who would pass for Americans and I have seen some girls among them who would be considered beautiful even at Savannah or Beatties Ford. They are much more intelligent than the men and seem to be very kindhearted. However at the battle of Palo Alto there were four hundred of these women on the ground with sharpened knives to mangle the bodies of the killed, wounded and captured. In fact the few of our men that fell into their hands were butchered by these devils in the shape of women, with the most infernal ferocity. By the way before these battles, the whole Mexican Army had taken the sacrament to give no quarter, not to spare the life of a single American. In all the Mexican towns there is in the centre of them a Plaza or great Square. This is the prettiest part* *of the town, the few good houses to be seen are in the Plaza, shade trees line the side of the squares and under these groups are always collected in good weather, smoking their shuck cigars, jabbering or sleeping. The houses in the suburbs are either of adobes, cane or crooked sticks. The people are in a deplorable state of ignorance, what little education they have is acquired from their priests, as they have no school-masters. They told us that their priests only visited the wealthy, that they were cruel & licentious, generally having five or six mistresses. I saw but one evidence of a religious spirit, a cross at one of the Ranchos with an inscription on it showing that a man had been murdered by the Cumanche Indians and praying that the Virgin might bless his soul. They told us that the cross had been blessed by the priest and as long as it was kept at the house of the deceased was as good as an incessant prayer for the rest of his soul. 'Tis a pity that this lovely country should be owned by people so sunk in ignorance and barbarism. There is as fine corn here as I ever saw and yet it has not been worked at all. They plant and let the Virgin take care of the growth. But little cotton is raised although it would grow most luxuriantly. I saw some finer than ever was seen in Carolina, although it had neither been plowed nor hoed. They are now planting their second crop, the first was much injured by the unusual flood in the rivers. This town is on the San Juan River about five miles from its junction with the Rio Grande. The town is on a very high bluff and yet it was overflowed and several hundred houses destroyed. I accidentally saw Albert at the mouth of the river (the Rio Grande) for a few moments. I was pained to see him but really could not help laughing at his boyish enthusiasm. I made him right mad by abusing the volunteers, laughing at his patriotism and advising him to go home. One thing is certain when these ardent young men get home again, they will not be silly enough to be caught volunteering again. The Mississippi Regiment will not be here for a month. I am with the Advance Guard of the Army and the company to which I belong is on the right of that Guard so that we have the post of honor of the whole "Army of Occupation." I hope*

Third Day of the Siege of Monterey by Sarony and Major

*we will not be unworthy of that trust. Things are in inextricable con-
fusion; we have not adequate transportation and 'tis impossible for us
to move forward until the last of September. I think of sending you on
my journal, it may possibly interest you. I have many warm friends here
and am delighted to be with them once more. Our encampment is on
a high dry bluff and is very healthy. I never felt better in my life. Thank
goodness we have no Volunteers among us and will have none for at
least a month. I have not yet heard from home. I would rather that you
wrote but seldom. Most of your letters will never reach me although you
will probably get the most of mine. I cannot bear the thought of your
letters being pried over at the dead letter office at Washington. Send me
a paper every two weeks. I care not how old & worthless it is. I will
know that all are well if it reaches me. If it does not, 'tis no matter. I
will write frequently myself. Neither myself no Mr. Ross have written,
at least I have not heard from you. Your affectionate son . . . You must
not let the girls think that a man in Mexico is the same as a man in the
grave. 'Tis no such thing, no such thing.*

    Remember me to all of the neighbors who may be kind enough to inquire for me. I am very proud of being with the Advance Corps and would be glad to move forward at any moment. Do not let the children forget me. I have written in great haste.

    D. H. H.

Although he left the army at the end of the war to teach mathematics at Washington College, Hill joined the Confederates early on and led his troops in many of the Civil War's major battles, including Antietam and Chickamauga. The brother-in-law of Mexican War veteran and Confederate general Robert E. Lee, Hill went on to hold such prominent positions as president of both the University of Arkansas and the Georgia Military Academy.

PRIVATE WERNER LIEBERT
TO HIS PARENTS,

German Army, December 1914,

World War I

One of the most astonishing acts of goodwill ever seen on a battlefield occurred during December 1914. Huddled and frozen in rain-soaked, muddy trenches, eating the same gruesome rations day in and day out, and with front lines often no more than 60 to 70 yards apart, soldiers must have been demoralized by the approaching holiday season. Surprisingly, minor acts of fraternization occurred between the opposing forces. Sometimes one side would shout insults to the other but later yell "Encore!" to encourage more holiday singing. These unusual contacts continued until the British corps commander, General Smith-Dorrien, felt compelled to issue a directive demanding that field officers encourage "the offensive spirit of the troops, while on the defensive, by every means in their power. Friendly intercourse with the enemy, unofficial armistices (e.g., 'we won't fire if you don't' etc.) and the exchange of tobacco and other comforts, however tempting and occasionally amusing they may be, are absolutely prohibited."

On December 7, 1914, Pope Benedict XV proposed a Christmas truce, something to which the Germans readily agreed. Despite the Allies' refusal to participate, many German units went ahead with their holiday celebrations, and British forward observers were shocked one day to notice hundreds of small, lighted Christmas trees perched on top of the trenches, accompanied by the singing of "O Tannenbaum" and other traditional carols. Gradually, a measure of trust was established and in many areas soldiers crawled out from their trenches, shook hands with the enemy,   showed pictures of loved ones, and exchanged cigarettes, stories, and souvenirs. In at least one documented case, the Bedfordshire Regiment and German soldiers played a game of soccer between their trenches, until their ball was punctured by barbed wire. The Christmas truce was declared for another reason: Both sides wished to recover their fallen comrades whose corpses were strewn across the bleak and cratered no-man's-land. The following letter by German soldier Werner Liebert was written during the truce.

★

My dear, dear parents —

Your letter of the 26th brought me the sad certainty that my dear brother had died a hero's death for Germany's victory. The post came early this morning.

My pain is inexpressible. I am not to be comforted. I can't yet realize that I shall not see Hans or hear his voice again. The thought that the dear fellow, who went off so full of joy and hope, will never again see that home and those dear ones for whom he was no doubt longing just as I am, is intolerable. Of you and your sorrow I cannot think without tears.

Only one thing comforts me a little: since I have known that my dear brother is no more, a wonderful change has taken place in me. I suddenly believe in immortality and in a meeting again in the other world. Those conceptions were empty words to me before. Since the day

. . . since I have known that my dear brother is no more . . . I suddenly believe in immortality and in a meeting again in the other world. Those conceptions were empty words to me before.

before yesterday they are objects of firm faith. For it cannot be that death should part one forever from those one loves. What would be the use of all love and affection, which are the most beautiful flowers in human life, if they were to be destroyed for ever in an instant? This is certainly but a small consolation for the fact that the poor fellow has been deprived of all his life's happiness. How beautiful life is one only realizes out here, where one has constantly to risk losing it. It was the clearest, most beautiful night we have had for a long time, just as still and pure as Christmas ought to be. It was freezing too, which put an end to the mud and filth. I thought much about home and was sorry you were not having a Christmas tree, because I wasn't able to picture what you were doing.

It was delightful to see the men all standing together while the names were read out and the parcels handed out over their heads. They were all real "Christmas children" as they knelt before the packages and burrowed into them—by a manager in a cow-house, as on the first "Holy Night."

In the evening we had our real Christmas celebration. There were two big trees, standing all lit up on big tables. We got everything we could possibly wish for: knitted comforts, tobacco, cake, chocolate, sausages—all "Love-Gifts".—What Germany has done for us! Then the Colonel and the Divisional Chaplain came in, the Bible story of Christmas was read and the dear old hymns were sung.

In some areas, this extraordinary holiday break lasted until New Year's Day 1915. Then the killing continued, Liebert falling on May 10, 1915. The 1914 Christmas truce was never repeated.

FIREMAN 1ST CLASS KEITH LYNCH
TO HIS FAMILY,

on board the USS <u>Rutilucus,</u> September 23, 1945,
World War II

This letter sent home by a 19-year-old sailor serving in the U.S. Navy is curiously connected to a more famous one written six years earlier on August 2, 1939, by Albert Einstein to President Franklin D. Roosevelt. In it, Einstein informed the president: "In the course of the last four months it has been made probable—through the work of Joliot in France as well as Fermi and Szilard in America—that it may become possible to set up a nuclear chain reaction in a large mass of uranium, by which vast amounts of power and large quantities of new radium-like elements would be generated. . . . This new phenomenon would also lead to the construction of bombs, and it is conceivable—though much less certain—that extremely powerful bombs of a new type may thus be constructed. A single bomb of this type, carried by boat and exploded in a port, might very well destroy the whole port. . . . such bombs might very well prove to be too heavy for transportation by air. . . ." Roosevelt was not handed Einstein's letter until October, at which time he established a "Uranium Committee" and approved an initial, albeit minor, appropriation of

$6,000 to purchase sufficient uranium and graphite for experimental use. The administration's reluctance to fund ongoing research continued until December 6, 1941, the day before Pearl Harbor was attacked, when it committed substantial resources to the effort, later dubbed the "Manhattan Project." Hitler, too, was not a believer in atomic weaponry—he bet his dwindling resources on the V-1 and V-2 missile program instead of on the atomic bomb research supervised by Werner Heisenberg.

On August 6, 1945, a nuclear weapon nicknamed Little Boy was detonated over Hiroshima, destroying the city and killing between 70,000 and 140,000 people, including 21 American POWs. When the Japanese failed to respond, a second bomb was unleashed on Nagasaki where an additional 35,000 to 70,000 people were slain. The Japanese surrendered unconditionally on August 14.

Dear Folks,

Here it is Sunday, Holiday Routine again. Boy, does the time fly. It seems as if it were only yesterday that I sat out here topside of the veranda and wrote the last time. We've gotten mail twice this week and I've my share, eight of them. The last one I got was mailed the 10th of September, the same day we left Okinawa. A letter in twelve days. That's not so bad. . . .

Well, to come to one of the two main topics I am to discuss (like they say in the movies): yesterday I went on my first, and most likely, only liberty in Nagasaki. The crew was divided into six sections and one went every hour. Each tour lasted two hours. We went to the beach and were put in trucks and given a tour of the city of Nagasaki. First we visited the main part of the city. It wasn't hurt so much by the atomic bomb. The only activity you see is people walking, going nowhere, it seems. Just walking. The only people doing anything were some men working on telephone lines. Everyone, even a quarter of the women, have on uniforms. Army, Navy, what appear to be WACs, Army and Navy cadets (about 8 to18 years old), etc. A lot of the younger boys carry what look to me like junior Sumari swords. A couple of us came close to relieving one of them of his sword. Or maybe bargain him out of it. But the chief persuaded us to forget it. Then we left that part of town and went to the other, the one that was hit by the bomb.

Now I know what they mean when they say a dead city. You remember when I first described the place to you? About the city being in two valleys going at right angles to each other from the harbor, with a string of mountains between them? The smaller of the two, about the same size and five or six times the population of Tecumseh, was the first we visited. It was damaged of course by the concussion of the atomic blast and also by two previous bombings. But the main part of the place, in the other valley, about the size of Lincoln I would say, and five or six times the population, was completely inundated. The sight I saw from the top of the hill, over which it was approximated the center of the blast, was a sight I hope my children, if I am so fortunate, will never have to see, hear of, or ever think of. It was horrible and when you got to thinking, unbelievable.

To think that a thirty-pound bomb the size of a basketball, exploding a thousand feet in the air, could cause such a holocaust was simply unbelievable. I shudder to think what these people underwent when the blast occurred. A blast that literally dissolved their homes, family, friends and any other material thing in the vicinity. A blast that pushed over huge steel structures a mile and a half away as if they were made of blocks. Now I can see what they mean when they say Dead City. A city with no buildings, no trees, no facilities, and no people. All you see from the top of the hill is a ground covered with bricks, burned wood, twisted and pushed over steel frames of buildings for several miles in each direction. There is nothing for the people of this Dead City to do *but walk around and think, "What manner of people would do such a thing to us, who are a peaceful, courteous and civilized people?" I wondered what they thought when they looked at us as we were driving along. "Are these the barbarians who did such a thing to us? What can we expect now that we are at their mercy?" I only wish they could be made to suffer a tenth of the atrocities that they performed on our men whom they held prisoner. People can say these people are simple, ignorant of the facts, or under a spell, but a nation cannot wage war as they have without the backing of the majority of their people.*

Such a thing as I saw yesterday cannot be described in words. You have to see it and I hope no one ever has to see such a thing again.

Well, today the occupation forces came into Nagasaki. The Sixth Marines, I think they are. If anyone ever says to someone from the Wichita Hospital Ship House or the USS Rutilicus *that they were the first to land on Nagasaki, that person will be viewing the world through what is known as a mouse, or breathing through what is known as a busted nose.*

Well, I found out that my enlistment expires next March. If I get out then it'll just about be right. Here's hoping. Well, folks, I've got a couple other letters to write before the movie. I'll see if I can't get another letter off before next Sunday.

Til then,

Love,

Son

Einstein, a devout pacifist, remained ignorant of how his letter to Roosevelt had influenced the U.S. government during the six years following its writing. Vacationing in Saranac Lake in the Adirondacks, he listened with horror to the radio reports about the destruction of Hiroshima and Nagasaki. Years later, he confided to his colleague and fellow Nobel laureate, Linus Pauling, "I made one great mistake in my life—when I signed a letter to President Roosevelt recommending that atom bombs be made."

LIEUTENANT RICHARD E. CRONAN
TO HIS MOTHER,

Suwon Air Force Base, Korea, December 8, 1951,

Korean War

The Lockheed F-80C "Shooting Star" was the first American jet fighter manufactured in large numbers and the first to exceed 500 mph. A descendant of aircraft designed at the close of World War II, it was a sturdy, single-seat, fixed-wing plane with a maximum speed of 577 mph and a range of 1,100 miles. The Shooting Star had six .50-caliber machine guns located in the plane's nose and could carry either twin 1,000-pound bombs on its wingtips, eight five-inch rockets, or 75 gallons of napalm. As good as the plane was, it was outclassed, as Cronan writes, by the Russian-built MIG-15. But in the world's first all-jet fighter air engagement, Lieutenant Russell Brown, flying an F-80C, shot down a MIG-15. However, due to its overall inferiority, the F-80C was reassigned to ground attack support.

Arrived in the Frozen Chosen [military nickname for Korea] a couple of days ago, the 6th to be exact. Cold as blue blazes. We are checking out

U.S. Air Force F-80C "Shooting Stars" heading toward Communist frontline positions in Korea

this week. Seems every group has its policy. We've been flying 80s [F-80 fighters] for 9 months; come over here to fly 80s and they put us through another check out, can't blame them though, they want to know what they are getting in their combat groups . . . a lot of men depend on one another. It has to be a closely-knit team or no one comes back to play again.

The spirit is fine around here. Mud about two inches deep. Ruts frozen solid at night. Tents cold despite the stove, airmen working long cold hours, pilots flying missions all day long and yet, like every fighter base, not a man would think of shirking his duties. The American fighting man can't be beat, I'm sure of that. One might lose a few battles now and then but never a war. We have inferior aircraft over here, not enough equipment for the pilots; but every man is a 'tiger' and scratch his name from a mission and you've never heard such fuss and hollering.

The MIGs [Soviet-made jet fighters] are really giving the boys a hard time as of the last month. Up to then it was flak and fifties and

The 80 is no match for the MIG. But, our boys have the fighting spirit, no doubt about it. . . . I'm on pins and needles waiting to get a crack at them.

small arms fire. Now the MIGs are hitting our formations as they come off the target.

The 80 is no match for the MIG. But, our boys have the fighting spirit, no doubt about it. If the MIGs come down the 80s turn into them and put up a scrap. I'm on pins and needles waiting to get a crack at them. Maybe next week. I drove my truck to Youngdong-po yesterday. The destruction is beyond description. Not a hut has been spared. Both sides have occupied this area twice and there ain't nothing left, let me tell you. But the people, the orphans cling to that spark of life somehow living in caves, huts. The homeless kids are a heart rending sight . . . rain, snow, no place to go, begging, no clothes, maybe a pair of shoes, no socks, little hands blue, bleeding, infected.

I'll be glad when they call it quits. But, while it is on, let me at 'em. Don't worry about me,

Dick

Cronan, a member of the 35th Fighter Bomber Squadron ("Black Panthers") attached to the 8th Fighter Bomber Wing, was shot down over Korea four days after writing this letter. His body was never recovered. The USAF Museum at Wright-Patterson Air Force Base has an F-80C from Cronan's fighter-bomber group on display.

CHIEF WARRANT OFFICER BRUCE McINNES TO HIS MOTHER,

Ban Me Thuot, South Vietnam, July 20, 1969,

Vietnam War

Bruce McInnes served with the 155th Assault Helicopter Company, based in Ban Me Thuot, South Vietnam, from May 1969 to December 1970, and his company's units were nicknamed Falcons and Stagecoach. The 155th was located in the II Tactical Zone and covered nearly 33,000 square miles, or almost half of South Vietnam.

In an interview, General Frederick C. Weyand, U.S. Army (retired), observed that some of his men in Vietnam had adopted "a local Catholic school . . . where their donations had bought textbooks, paid teachers' salaries, and provided school lunches for the children. Ten days later, the unit that had been in Boi Loi was conducting training programs, and the unit that had been at the school was beating the bush. One day they were safe, watching little children at school; the next, they were in mortal danger, watching for someone to pop out of the ground and try to kill them. It's hard to put in words what a terrible burden that imposed. You had to go through it to fully understand the incredible psychological strain they were under. It was a hell of a burden our soldiers in Vietnam had to bear. . . . I guess that during my five years in Vietnam, I paid more than a thousand visits to U.S. units in the field. And in almost every case, they would begin their briefing with an account of what they had been doing to help the villagers in their area—medical team visits; help to local churches, schools and orphanages; road building, construction assistance, and the like. For every terrible aberration like My Lai, there were thousands of acts of charity and compassion. Yet you would never know that from what was reported here at home."

Dear Mom,

I've become involved recently in a situation that I had heard about but was never fully aware of before. I thought, as a child, that growing up in a single-parent family was rough. Now I know that I was very well off compared to those with no parents at all, no home life to build a healthy young life on. I think of something in the Bible, "I cried because I had no shoes, and then I saw a man who had no feet."

Let me start from the beginning. When I first arrived in Vietnam, and was assigned here in Ban Me Thuot, I was astonished at the poor, seemingly unimprovable conditions that the majority of Vietnamese live under. True, over the last three decades new conveniences [and] new ideas have been introduced by us and the French before us. [But] I had to talk with the people before I realized that the sole hope of this nation lies in its youth. The elders, the parents, are tired. They've lived with war, and the hardships involved, for too long. They no longer believe another kind of life is possible. The children do, though. They want to learn. They want to do things the way we do, have things like we have. They have hope for their future.

One day when I wasn't scheduled to fly, my platoon leader, Capt. Roy Ferguson, asked me if I wanted to go to the orphanage in town with him. We picked up some things some friends had sent him and went down to the Vinh-Son Orphanage and School, run by eight sisters of the Daughters of Charity of St. Vincent de Paul.

Sister Beatrice, in charge of the school, greeted us at the gate. As we walked through the grounds, we were followed by scores of children who wanted to touch us, talk to us, or just smile at us. We left the books and pencils we had brought with Sister Beatrice and walked to the building which is the orphanage itself.

We were welcomed by Sister Helen and a group of kids that had been playing in front of the building. They just went wild when they saw us. And no wonder—for the past five months, Capt. Ferguson, who comes from Wyalusing, Pennsylvania, has been practically their only link with the life of clothing, toys and personal American friendship. They've adopted him, in their own way, as a sort of godfather.

I was at once ashamed and proud. Proud because we in America have so much, and ashamed because we take our good fortune for granted, wasting so much that these people, especially the children in this orphanage so desperately need. Things like blankets and sheets, clothes for little boys and girls, even shoes. How many times have you or I made a rag out of something because it had a little hole in it? Mom, these children need those things desperately. Capt. Ferguson will be leaving soon, and I will sort of assume the privilege of being the go-between for these children and the assistance that comes in from their friends in the United States... The most beneficial thing we can do is donate our time by going down to the school to teach English to the more than 1,200 students that receive an education there.

I'm amazed that eight nuns can oversee so large an effort. In addition to the orphanage and school, they run a dispensary, giving aid to the local Vietnamese and Montagnard families in the area. They have so little for themselves, and yet they give away what they do have.

The shame of it all is that these children had nothing to do with bringing all this on themselves. It's hard to sympathize with someone

. . . these children had nothing to do with bringing all this on them-selves. It's hard to sympathize with someone who causes his own mis-fortune. These children, though, are the victims not of their generation, but of yours and mine.

who causes his own misfortune. These children, though, are the victims not of their generation, but of yours and mine. Many are orphans because their parents have been killed. They haven't died of old age or heart attacks…they've been killed by terrorism while defending their homes, their country, their freedom. Others are orphans as a result of the assistance we have given to their country. We have fathered many children, unable to take them home, their mothers unable to care for them. You and I must do something for these children, for this orphanage, [so it] can expand its work and care for children who now walk the streets with no one, no one at all.

The children need things that are part of our everyday lives. Toothpaste, soap, a pencil, a pen, a notebook to write in as they go through school. A picture book that says, "See the dog. His name is Spot. Watch the dog run. Run, Spot, run." These kids aren't underprivileged —they're nonprivileged, and they're running. Running towards a way

A U.S. Air Force dental officer examines the teeth of one of the
more than 150 orphans at Lac Thien orphanage

*of life where they can better themselves on their own. But they're so
young, we have to help them to walk before we let them run.*

*Plates on which to put their food, silverware to eat it with, even the
food itself—they need it all. They raise chickens and pigs, and all of
their vegetables. The only way they can buy even rice is to sell one of
their pigs. [The children] are taught by a staff of 30 teachers who work
for nothing or are paid in produce. There's no law here requiring children to attend school. They go because they are hungry for knowledge
and because their stomachs are hungry. An education can change that,
and we must help them get that education.*

I could write a book about these children, about the look of fear in their eyes, their cries of joy upon seeing an American, someone who can help them change their circumstances. Some are too young to fully realize what it's like to have nothing. You and I and our friends must prevent them from finding out. We speak different languages, but we're all the same kind of people. They need, and we have. We must help them.

I'll stop here, because the sooner this letter gets to you, the sooner our friends at the orphanage will get some help. Send anything that might be useful to Vinh Son Orphanage care of myself. I'll see that it gets there. And don't be surprised if the next piece of mail you get from Vietnam is a thank-you note from some very, very grateful Vietnamese youngster.

Run, Spot, run.

With love and thanks,
Your Son

MATTHEW TO HIS FATHER, MAJOR THOMAS A. DEALL

United States of America,

Operation Enduring Freedom

On September 11, 2001, my life in New York, like the lives of so many others across the country, was thrown into chaos. I kept thinking about my 4-year-old son, Jacob, and if he could be protected from . . . I didn't know what. Weeks later, my wife and I still struggled to find a way to explain to our child what had happened. Why were there so many racing fire trucks, police cars, and wailing sirens? he asked. Why were pictures of people plastered on building walls? What were the banners and flowers at firehouses for? We so much wanted to protect his innocence and in so doing, protect what was left of ours.

At the time of the attacks, Major Deall was in Germany, filling a staff officer position within the U.S. European Command's personnel directorate. Having served for seven months during Desert Shield/Desert Storm, he understands how important it is to maintain communication with family and friends back home through letters, e-mails, phone calls, and so on. An e-mail from his 12-year-old son, who had been diagnosed with epilepsy only two months earlier, helped him appreciate a child's perspective of the events.

Dad,

After receiving a very good letter, I still feel bad about you being gone and what is going on today. Today I spoke to the school counselor, which made me feel like a baby because, I'm a tough big giant overweight hockey player who cries more than he smiles! I try to talk about happy things, but with all that is going on I can't think of one happy thought. I only wish I could, but I don't think I'm brave enough to do that. I only wish that you were not in the military. But then I would have to feel like an ordinary person who has to worry about nothing. But now I understand that you're doing this under a good oath. I remember in the movie, The Rock, the soldier said before he died, "I will protect this country from enemies foreign and domestic." And then I heard mom say that this is why your father wears that uniform. And it brought tears to my eyes hearing mom say that and seeing those American soldiers die in the line of fire. I so much wish I could get over the fact that I have epilepsy and now can't wear the uniform or be a pilot, but I can't. At night I pray that I didn't have epilepsy and could fly for the USAF, but I have power over nothing. And I wish you were here. I remember saying one line with you from the movie Armageddon 'I want to go shopping.' Then I would say, 'Me too!' Making me laugh was always your specialty and still is. And going back to the sayings part,

I only wish that you were not in the military. But then I would have to feel like an ordinary person who has to worry about nothing.

I remember that President Bush said, 'As I walk through the shadow of death, I fear no evil.' That is what made me think. And there is a song that plays over here from a band called The Calling. The song is called "Turn Back Time." I wish I could turn back time and stop this. Like I said in my last letter, I've never cried so much in my life. And I feel stupid about crying because I'm a big boy who plays rough hockey and I can't cry. Then today I realized that Ray Bourque cried. But he cried over victory. To me, this is not a victory.

I need you to call and tell me it's OK to cry and that it's OK to talk to people and just tell me it's OK. I love you, dad.

Your son, Matthew

Letters from Leaders

PRESIDENT ABRAHAM LINCOLN
TO MAJOR GENERAL JOSEPH HOOKER,

Washington, D.C., January 26, 1863,

Civil War

F ighting Joe," a nickname he abhorred, was the third general Lincoln appointed to lead the Army of the Potomac, succeeding generals George B. McClellan and Ambrose E. Burnside. Lincoln was not entirely pleased with Hooker's abilities. The existence of this letter, which historian Robert G. Ingersoll praised as having "no parallel," remained unknown until after the general's death in 1879. If Lincoln had doubts about Hooker's command, they were reinforced less than four months later by his loss to General Robert E. Lee at Chancellorsville. In 1863, shortly before the Battle of Gettysburg, Hooker was replaced by General George G. Meade. Hooker served as a corps commander in the Department of the West, but his military career never fully recovered. Passed over at General Sherman's orders by General Oliver Howard to head the Army of Tennessee, Hooker requested and was granted relief from duty. He did, however, lead Lincoln's funeral procession through Springfield, Illinois, on May 4, 1865.

*I have heard, in such way as to
believe it, of your recently saying
that both the Army and the
Government needed a Dictator.
Of course it was not for this, but
in spite of it, that I have
given you the command.*

General:

I have placed you at the head of the Army of the Potomac. Of course I have done this upon what appear to me to be sufficient reasons. And yet I think it best for you to know that there are some things in regard to which, I am not quite satisfied with you. I believe you to be a brave and skilful soldier, which, of course, I like. I also believe you do not mix politics with your profession, in which you are right. You have confidence in yourself, which is a valuable, if not an indispensable quality. You are ambitious, which, within reasonable bounds, does good rather than harm. But I think that during Gen. Burnside's command of the Army you have taken counsel of your ambition, and thwarted him as much as you could, in which you did a great wrong to the country, and to a most meritorious and honorable brother officer. I have heard, in such way as to believe it, of your recently saying that both the Army and

(Opposite): General Joseph Hooker

the Government needed a Dictator. Of course it was not for this, but in spite of it, that I have given you the command. Only those generals who gain successes, can set up dictators. What I now ask of you is military success, and I will risk the dictatorship. The government will support you to the utmost of its ability, which is neither more nor less than it has done and will do for all commanders. I much fear that the spirit which you have aided to infuse into the Army, of criticising their Commander and withholding confidence from him, will now turn upon you. I shall assist you as far as I can, to put it down. Neither you, nor Napoleon, if he were alive again, could get any good out of an army, while such a spirit prevails in it. And now, beware of rashness. Beware of rashness, but with energy, and sleepless vigilance, go forward and give us victories.

Yours very truly,

A. Lincoln

COLONEL THEODORE ROOSEVELT TO HIS DAUGHTER ALICE,

near Santiago, Cuba, July 18, 1898,

Spanish-American War

R oosevelt wrote this touching and revealing note to his oldest daughter, 14-year-old Alice, just one day after the fall of Santiago (which virtually ended the Spanish-American War) and 17 days following his famous charge up San Juan Hill. His only child from his first marriage to Alice Hathaway Lee, Alice and her father were very close, in part because of a shared tragedy. On Valentine's Day 1884, just two days after Alice's birth, both Roosevelt's wife and mother passed away. Two years later, T.R. married his childhood sweetheart, Edith Kermit Carow, who bore him five additional children. These highly spirited youngsters, and Alice in particular, led Roosevelt to observe, "I can be President of the United States, or I can control Alice. I cannot possibly do both."

Darling Alice,

I was very glad to get your letter, and to hear of all you had done. I have had a very hard and dangerous month. I have enjoyed it, too, in

My men are not well fed, and they are fierce and terrible in battle; but they [gave] half they had to the poor women and children.

a way; but war is a grim and fearful thing. It is strange to see "Nicanor lie dead in his harness," when Nicanor and you have that morning spoken together with eager longing of glory and honor to be won or lost, and of the loved ones who will be thrilled or struck down according as the event of the day goes. Worse still is the awful agony of the field hospital where the wounded lie day and night in the mud, drenched with rain and scorched with the terrible sun; while the sky overhead is darkened by the whirling vultures and the stream of staring fugitives, the poor emaciated women and the little tots of children, some like Archie and Quentin [Roosevelt's two youngest sons]. One poor little mite still carried a canary in a little cage. My men are not well fed, and they are fierce and terrible in battle; but they [gave] half they had to the poor women and children. I suppose a good many of them thought, as I did, of their own wives or sisters and little ones. War is often, as this one is, necessary and righteous; but it is terrible.

Your loving father

T.R.

(Opposite): Alice Roosevelt

As the independent-minded and often obstreperous Alice grew older, she lost none of her rebellious spirit. Observing her father's constant need to be the center of attention, she quipped that he wanted "to be the bride at every wedding and the corpse at every funeral." On February 17, 1906, Alice married Ohio congressman Nicholas Longworth in one of the most lavish weddings ever held at the White House. During her lifetime, "Princess" Alice grew to be such a fixture on the capital scene that she was known as "the other Washington Monument." Well into her 70s, she was even available to assist Jacqueline Kennedy in restoring the White House in the early 1960s. She died a week following her ninety-sixth birthday, and her epitaph could well have been her favorite maxim, reportedly embroidered on a pillow: "If you can't say something good about someone, sit right here by me."

PRESIDENT FRANKLIN D. ROOSEVELT TO MR. AND MRS. SULLIVAN,

Washington, D.C., February 2, 1943,

World War II

The USS *Juneau* (CL-52) was built by the Federal Shipbuilding Co. of Kearny, New Jersey, and launched on October 25, 1941, under the command of Captain Lyman K. Swenson. Described as a "Super Destroyer," the *Juneau* was the first ship painted in camouflage and carried 16 five-inch guns, 8 torpedo tubes, depth charges, and machine guns. Departing for the Pacific on August 22, 1942, she first saw action near the Santa Cruz Islands on October 26, and for her conduct during that battle, particularly against attacking Japanese fighter planes, she was nicknamed "the Mighty J." The *Juneau* continued to provide superior protection to U.S. forces deployed to reinforce Guadalcanal.

In an engagement with the Japanese navy on November 13, the *Juneau* was struck on its port side by a torpedo and forced to withdraw from the fight—her bow was down 12 feet, and her speed reduced to 13 knots. A short while later, a second torpedo slammed into the same section and split the ship in half. She sank in less than a minute, taking down Captain Swenson and 550 crew members, among them five brothers named Sullivan from Waterloo, Iowa,

the five Sullivan brothers
"missing in action" off the Solomons

THEY DID THEIR PART

who had enlisted and asked to serve on the same ship after a friend died at Pearl Harbor. One hundred fifty men managed to escape, but rescue efforts were delayed by a week, and by then only ten survivors were fished out of the open sea. Tragically, also on board the *Juneau* were four brothers from the Roger family, and three from the Combs family.

The *Juneau* received four battle stars for her World War II service. President Franklin D. Roosevelt, a former assistant secretary of the navy, wrote the Sullivan brothers' parents.

My Dear Mr. and Mrs. Sullivan:

The knowledge that your five gallant sons are missing in action against the enemy inspired me to write you this personal message. I realize full well there is little I can say to assuage your grief.

As the Commander-in-Chief of the Army and the Navy, I want you to know that the entire nation shares in your sorrow. I offer you the condolence and gratitude of our country. We who remain to carry on the fight must maintain the spirit, in the knowledge that such sacrifice is not in vain.

The Navy Department has informed me of the expressed desire of your sons, George Thomas, Francis Henry, Joseph Eugene, Madison Abel, and Albert Leo, to serve on the same ship. I am sure that we all take heart in the knowledge that they fought side by side. As one of your sons wrote, "We will make a team together that can't be beat." It is this spirit which in the end must triumph.

Last March you, Mrs. Sullivan, were designated to sponsor a ship of the Navy, in recognition of your patriotism and that of your sons. I am to understand that you are now even more determined to carry on as sponsor. This evidence of unselfishness and of courage serves as a real inspiration for me, as I am sure it will for all Americans. Such acts of faith and fortitude in the face of tragedy convince me of the indomitable spirit and will of our people.

I send you my deepest sympathy in your hour of trial and pray that in Almighty God you will find a comfort and help that only He can bring.

Very sincerely yours,

Franklin D. Roosevelt

Despite their tragic loss, Thomas and Alleta Sullivan and one of their daughters continued to support the war effort. They visited more than 200 production plants and shipyards, encouraging workers to produce more weapons and help shorten the conflict. By January 1944, the family had spoken to more than a million laborers in 65 cities. Millions heard their story on the radio, and in 1944, *The Fighting Sullivans,* a movie directed by Lloyd Bacon, was released. The fate of the Sullivan brothers also inspired the recent Steven Spielberg hit, *Saving Private Ryan.* On February 10, 1943, at President Roosevelt's order, the Navy renamed a destroyer under construction *The Sullivans.* After it was decommissioned in 1965, a second ship, a guided-missile destroyer with the same name, was launched on August 12, 1995, christened by one of the brother's granddaughters.

PRESIDENT HARRY TRUMAN
TO IRV KUPCINET OF
THE CHICAGO SUN-TIMES,

Independence, Missouri, August 5, 1963,

World War II

On July 16, 1945, the first atomic bomb was detonated in the Alamogordo Desert of New Mexico. That test was the culmination of years of research and massive funding. But now the decision whether to use the most powerful explosive device ever developed rested in the hands of Harry Truman, president for only three months since the death of Franklin D. Roosevelt. Although the war was winding down, there was no clear-cut indication that the Japanese would agree to an unconditional surrender.

Truman noted in his diary on July 25, 1945: "This weapon is to be used against Japan between now and August 10. I have told the secretary of war, Mr. Stimson, to use it so that military objectives and soldiers and sailors are the target and not women and children. Even if the Japs are savages, ruthless, merciless, and fanatic, we as the leader of the world for the common welfare cannot drop this terrible bomb on the old capital [Kyoto] or the new [Tokyo]. He and I are in accord. The target will be a purely military one, and we will issue a warning statement asking the Japs to surrender and save lives." The following day the United States broadcast its demand

HARRY S. TRUMAN
INDEPENDENCE, MISSOURI
August 5, 1963

Dear Kup:

I appreciated most highly your column of July 30th, a copy of which you sent me.

I have been rather careful not to comment on the articles that have been written on the dropping of the bomb for the simple reason that the dropping of the bomb was completely and thoroughly explained in my Memoirs, and it was done to save 125,000 youngsters on the American side and 125,000 on the Japanese side from getting killed and that is what it did. It probably also saved a half million youngsters on both sides from being maimed for life.

You must always remember that people forget, as you said in your column, that the bombing of Pearl Harbor was done while we were at peace with Japan and trying our best to negotiate a treaty with them.

All you have to do is to go out and stand on the keel of the Battleship in Pearl Harbor with the 3,000 youngsters under-neath it who had no chance whatever of saving their lives. That is true of two or three other battleships that were sunk in Pearl Harbor. Altogether, there were between 3,000 and 6,000 youngsters killed at that time without any declaration of war. It was plain murder.

I knew what I was doing when I stopped the war that would have killed a half million youngsters on both sides if those bombs had not been dropped. I have no regrets and, under the same circumstances, I would do it again - and this letter is not confidential.

Sincerely yours,

Harry Truman

Mr. Irv Kupcinet
Chicago Sun-Times
Chicago, Illinois

that Japan surrender completely or face annihilation. Despite intense firebombing, Japan still held on. Two days later, the Japanese premier rejected the Allied ultimatum out of hand as "unworthy of notice," but there is evidence to suggest that had the United States dropped its condition that Emperor Hirohito abdicate, Japan would have capitulated. Given the mood at the time—would the Allies have agreed to let Hitler stay in power, even if only as a figurehead?—the continued loss of life and the revelation of Japanese atrocities against American prisoners of war, it seems unlikely that Truman or the Allies would have found a conditional surrender acceptable. The following letter details Truman's decision to drop the bomb.

★

Dear Kup,

I appreciated most highly your column of July 30th, a copy of which you sent me.

I have been rather careful not to comment on the articles that have been written on the dropping of the bomb for the simple reason that the dropping of the bomb was completely and thoroughly explained in my Memoirs, and it was done to save 125,000 youngsters on the American side and 125,000 on the Japanese side from getting killed and that is what it did. It probably also saved a half million youngsters on both sides from being maimed for life.

You must always remember that people forget, as you said in your column, that the bombing of Pearl Harbor was done while we were at peace with Japan and trying our best to negotiate a treaty with them.

All you have to do is to go out and stand on the keel of the Battleship in Pearl Harbor with the 3,000 youngsters underneath it who had no chance whatever of saving their lives. That is true of two or three other battleships that were sunk in Pearl Harbor. Altogether, there were between 3,000 and 6,000 youngsters killed at that time without any declaration of war. It was plain murder.

I knew what I was doing when I stopped the war that would have killed a half million youngsters on both sides if those bombs had not been dropped. I have no regrets and, under the same circumstances, I would do it again—and this letter is not confidential.

Sincerely yours,

Harry S Truman

GENERAL COLIN POWELL
TO A 4TH-GRADE CLASS
Washington, D.C., 1991,
Gulf War

Kids say the darndest things," observed television host and author Art Linkletter. Well, kids occasionally *write* the darndest things, too, and sometimes they receive interesting responses, especially when the responses come from a country's leader. The most famous letter from a U.S. president to a child must be Abraham Lincoln's reply to 11-year-old Grace Bedell's note from October 14, 1860. In it, Grace writes to "A B Lincoln" suggesting that he let his whiskers grow, adding, "you would look a great deal better for your face is so thin. All the ladies like whiskers, and they would tease their husband's to vote for you and then you would be President." Lincoln replied right away, "As to the whiskers, having never worn any, do you not think people would call it a piece of silly affection if I were to begin it now?" Well, the rest, as they say, is history—Lincoln grew the whiskers *and* became president!

Another political leader with a beard even larger than Lincoln's also wrote to a president as a youngster. There is no indication, however, that President Franklin D. Roosevelt, addressed as "My good friend Roosevelt," ever answered the handwritten letter from

I did not want the war with Iraq to start, but when Iraq invaded Kuwait, Mr. Saddam Hussein started the war. The United Nations gave him over 5 months to withdraw his army. When he did not withdraw, we made him withdraw.

a 12-year-old boy from Santiago, Cuba, on November 6, 1940, who wrote in part, "If you like, give me a ten dollar bill green American, in the letter, because never, I have not seen a ten dollar bill green American and I would like to have one of them. . . ." Would the world have turned out differently had F. D. R. sent young Fidel Castro a $10 bill?

Colin Powell, America's first African American to be chairman of the Joint Chiefs of Staff and secretary of state, took the time to answer these questions from schoolchildren.

Dear Students:

Thank you for your letters and drawings. And, most of all thank you for your kind words and for your overwhelming support of our men and women in the armed forces.

I counted 16 questions! So, let me see if I can answer them for you.

1. It is exciting and a great challenge to be President Bush's top military advisor.

2. I feel very fortunate to be the son of Jamaican immigrants. My parents were two very wonderful people who imparted to me a set of values that I treasure.

3. I am married. My wife's name is Alma. I have three children. Michael, my son, is in law school at Georgetown University. Through Michael and his wife I have a grandson, Jeffrey. My daughter, Linda, is an actress living in New York City. My daughter, Annemarie, is a student at William and Mary College.

4. Yes, I am very glad the war is over.

5. I enjoy being a general because I get to work with troops anywhere. It always raises my morale to meet with men and women of our armed forces.

6. I live in quarters No. 6 at Fort Myer, Virginia. From my house I can see the Washington Monument, the Lincoln Memorial, the Jefferson Memorial and other Washington sights.

7. I was in Vietnam twice, once in 1962–63 and again in 1968–69.

8. My birthday is 5 April and I am 54 years old.

9. I did not want the war with Iraq to start, but when Iraq invaded Kuwait, Mr. Saddam Hussein started the war. The United Nations gave him over 5 months to withdraw his army. When he did not withdraw, we made him withdraw.

10. I was awarded the Purple Heart when I was wounded by a booby-trap in Vietnam.

11. I was appointed by President Bush to be the 12th Chairman of the Joint Chiefs of Staff and I took office on October 1, 1989.

12. Yes, this was the first time General Schwarzkopf and I worked directly together in a war, although both of us fought in Vietnam as well.

13. I don't have a favorite color or food—there are so many of both that I like.

14. My best hobby is rebuilding old cars.

15. Yes, I think being a general is exciting, challenging, and it gives you an opportunity to work with some outstanding people.

16. Yes, General Schwarzkopf is a superb gentleman. I've always enjoyed working with him.

Now that I've answered your questions, let me ask a favor of each one of you. Study hard, do your homework, be kind to one another, and always remember that in America your dreams can come true.

Sincerely,

Colin L. Powell
Chairman
Joint Chiefs of Staff

Prisoners of War

PRIVATE LEWIS M. BRYANT TO THE <u>OTSEGO REPUBLICAN</u>,

Butternuts, New York, January 6, 1865,

Civil War

A t the begining of the Civil War, the North and South established a prisoner exchange system. But as the war dragged on,
the system collapsed, and both sides unexpectedly found
themselves forced to provide care and shelter for the soldiers they
had captured. The methods for housing these prisoners varied
widely, with the South deciding to move part of its growing prisoner population away from Richmond, Virginia, to a more secure
location. Shortly after its construction in Georgia in 1864,
Andersonville prison, officially known as Camp Sumter, became
the largest stockade in the Confederacy. Designed to hold 10,000
men, by August 1864 its population had swelled to nearly 33,000.
In its 14 months of operation, more than 45,000 prisoners of war
were incarcerated under deplorable circumstances, as the following
letter attests. With hundreds dying daily, conditions only worsened;
13,000 men died of malnutrition, disease, and exposure. The
morgue, called the deadhouse, was so filled with bodies that additional corpses were piled up like cordwood as they awaited burial—
many of them in mass graves. Guards watched from "pigeon roosts"

and shot at anyone attempting to cross the "deadline." Walt Whitman observed, "The dead there are not to be pitied as much as some of the living that have come from there—if they can be called living."

The following letter is written by a former Union prisoner of Andersonville to an editor of a New York newspaper.

Dear Sir:

Having spent over three years in "Dixie," and the last 5 months in the notorious confederate prison on my return many rebel sympathizers ready to charge falsehood upon the published accounts of the horrible sufferings experienced by the wretched inmates of that prison, and being pretty well known myself throughout this community, I beg you publish a short extract of my experience; and if any man knowing me shall doubt the truth of what I say, and wishes proof, I will pay his passage to Andersonville, petition the devil in charge to grant him admission, and if living and converted at the end of five months, I shall pay over to him all that I have received for services while in the army, and recommend him to Jeff Davis as a copperhead worthy of full fellowship.

I belong to the Second N.Y. Heavy Artillery. I was taken prisoner near Bottoms Bridge, Va. June 13, 1864. We were marched to Richmond, Va., robbed of our money, blankets and most of our clothes, and confined in Libby prison for eight days. Nothing occurred here worthy of note. We were crowded into a large room and lived on corn bread and water. The air being foul and almost suffocating. I, on one occasion, put my face to the grated window for relief, and was fired at by the guard outside, the ball just grazing my ear. I then learned that a breath of air at that window had cost many a poor boy his life.

On the 21st day of June about 8,000 of us were packed in box cars as closely as we could stand, like so many cattle for market, and started for Andersonville. We were seven days on the road—the distance by rail is about one-thousand miles—and we had but two rations of food or water during the passage. On the 28th we arrived at Andersonville. The prison is a field of twenty-five acres, mostly of wet, marshy ground, surrounded by a fence or stockade as it is called, built up of square timbers, close and tight about twenty feet high. We found in it thirty thousand prisoners the addition of our company making thirty-eight thousand. As we entered this place of cruelty, starvation and death, I shall never forget the heart-sickening picture that presented itself as I cast my eyes over the twenty-five acres of filthy, ragged, naked, lousy, sick and starving mass of still living human skeletons. Thousands were without hat or shoes; many without coat, vest or shirt, and others as naked as Adam before the fall. Some were shouting, some praying, some cursing, some crying for food, some weeping, and some whose sufferings had crazed the brain were fighting their comrades and giving orders for battle, under the supposition that they were charging on the rebel army.

I thought of Milton's pandemonium and felt that it must be a paradise compared with this.

As we entered the broad gate and looked upon this horrid scene, a companion of mine, heart-sickened and trembling in every limb, looking up to me with tearful eyes, and voice choking with emotion, asked (in the language of a poem I have since seen) "for God's sake, Bryant, is this hell?" And I thought it no wonder that the poor boy asked, for he had never before seen such a mass of pitiable, suffering objects on earth. But he was not destined to stay for long in son loathsome a place, for a few weeks after, overcome by starvation and disease, he yielded his body to the malice of those barbarous rebels, and his freed, happy spirit soared to the home of the patriot.

We marched into the crowd and the gate closed after us—to thousands the gate of death. We were then left to make the acquaintance of our new associates, listen to their tales of horror, and as appeared to us all, to prepare to die. We were allowed rations once a day, and this con-

sisted of a few ounces of corn meal to each man, and that ground with the cob—about half enough for one meal. This was given to us raw and without salt or other seasoning, with one stick of pine wood about fourteen inches long with which to cook it. This we mixed with water, and some times succeeded in cooking, or rather warming it, and at other times ate it entirely cold and raw. The water we obtained from a slough or swamp in one end of our pen where an old barrel had been sunk to keep out as much as possible the surrounding filth and mire.

    The filth, manure and mire all about our "springs" or "wells" as well called them, being at all times knee deep and the water that we drank was always and unavoidably filthy and full of worms and maggots. It was not an uncommon thing in the morning, as we went for water, to find some poor fellow dead in this swamp who had made an effort to reach the water and had sunk down in exhaustion, unable to ford the mire. There was not a tree or bush in the whole field to shade us from the scorching sun or shelter us from the storm. The fence or stockade might have afforded a shade in the middle of the day to a few, but if a poor fellow thought he were sick and dying, approached ti within twenty feet of it, he was, without notice or warning, shot by the inhuman guard, who were constantly watching such opportunities from their stations on the stockade. Many provided themselves with shelter from the sun and cold night winds by digging with their hands holes in the ground, something like a grave, large enough to receive them. I had the good fortune to be the owner of about one-half of an old blanket that fell to me on the death of a friend—Smith Cook of New Berlin, Chenengo county. I was considered a wealthy man on receipt of this, and was greatly envied by many of my companions. I turned this to be the best account possible. As it would partially cover three persons. I each night invited two companions to sleep with me. We then selected as dry a spot of ground as we could find unoccupied, lay together "spoon-fashion." our much coveted blanket over us, and slid off into dreams of home, feather-beds and mother's mince pies. But my blanket was final-

ly stolen from me, and I then knew what it was to be poor.

Our first business in the morning after breakfast, (if any had a breakfast to eat. I always ate my twenty-four hours ration for supper and fasted through the day,) was to carry out on a board for burial those of our companions who had died during the night. The number of deaths during the five months that I was there averaged one hundred and twenty per day. I counted them for one month. Some days there were as many as one hundred and fifty; and these all died, I know from exposure and starvation, for when they entered that hell of rebellion they were as hale and hearty a set of fellows as I ever saw together. When any of our company died, their clothing, if they had any, was taken to cover the living who were destitute. IN comparison with many others I was well dressed, and was considered quite a dandy, yet I should hardly be willing to appear in church at home in my Andersonville toilet. For five months I had neither hat, shoes, stockings, coat, vest or shirt, but I had a part of a pair of pants, which hung in strings, loose and airy, and the back of an old blouse, the front and sleeves having previously been honorably discharged from the service. Negroes were kept constantly at work digging trenches in which to bury our dead. After we had deposited them in piles outside the gate, they were thrown by the rebels and Negroes into a large six-mule wagon, carted by loads to the trenches, thrown in amid the scoffs and jeers of the rebels, without regard even to decency, and left to sleep till the great day of final accounts. As I have said before, all the men were filthy, ragged or naked, and swarmed with vermin. The limbs of many were palsied and stiff with scurvy. Some of them were swollen by dropsy almost to bursting. Thousands were seen whose bones pierced through the tightly drawn flesh—reduced by starvation—and sores formed at the hips, shoulder blades, etc. were filled with slimy maggots, whose every motion was untold agony to the unhappy sufferers who had not the strength to remove them. No care was taken of these martyrs, no medicine given, not attempt made to relieve them. They died by hundreds, to be buried like brutes. And all because they loved their country and fought for their flag. It is believed by the prisoners and sometimes admitted by our guard to be the policy of the rebels, to starve in prisons those that they cannot kill upon the field—that such as do not die in their hands shall be so utterly broken down as not be able again to lift their muskets against them. And it will never be better until the southern confederacy experiences religion, or our government adopt the system of retaliation—two things not likely to occur. But I am making my letter too long.

On the 25th day of November, about seven thousand of the sick and those nearest starved to death, were paroled and taken to Savannah to be send on board of our vessels, hundreds of whom died on the way. But when we came in sight of the glorious stars and stripes, there went up to heaven three as hearty cheers as were ever heard. Such as were too far gone to speak loud, whispered "hurrah!" and "thank God."

I am not an educated man nor skilled with the pen, but if I were, and understood all languages, I could not half express the sufferings of the prisoners in Georgia. And if the devil does not have the authors on their misery, I really cannot see the use of having any devil at all.

Very Truly yours,

Lewis M. Bryant

CAPTAIN HENRY WIRZ
TO PRESIDENT ANDREW JOHNSON,
Old Capitol Prison, Washington, D.C.,
November 6, 1865, Civil War

After receiving his medical degree from colleges in Paris and Berlin, Swiss-born Henry Wirz immigrated to the United States and opened a medical practice in Kentucky in 1849. At the beginning of the Civil War, Wirz enlisted in the 4th Battalion, Louisiana Volunteers, and was badly wounded at the Battle of Seven Pines in May 1862. Unable to serve in combat, he was appointed acting adjutant general to General John Winder, provost marshal for Confederate prisoner of war camps. On March 27, 1864, after working in prisons in Virginia and Alabama, Captain Wirz was assigned to Andersonville, remaining there until the war's end. After a short-lived retirement, Wirz was arrested on May 7, 1865, and transported three days later to the Old Capitol Prison to await trial on charges of conspiring with former Confederate president Jefferson Davis to "injure the health and destroy the lives of soldiers in the military service of the United States." The public was furious about the atrocious living conditions in Andersonville, and, despite blatant inconsistencies in some allegations, Wirz was convicted on all charges after a trial of nine weeks. Four days before his scheduled execution, Wirz wrote to President Andrew Johnson.

Mr. President:

With a trembling hand, with a heart filled with the most conflicting emotions, and with a spirit hopeful one moment and despairing the next, I have taken the liberty of addressing you. When I consider your exalted position; when I think for a moment that in your hands rests the weal and woe of millions—yea, the peace of the world—well may I pause to call to my aid courage enough to lay before you my humble petition. I have heard you spoken of as a man ready and willing at all times and under all circumstances to do justice, and that no man, however humble he may be, need fear to approach you: and, therefore, have come to the conclusion that you will allow me the same privilege as extended to hundreds and thousands of others. It is not my desire to enter into an argument as to the merits of my case. In your hands, if I am rightfully informed, are all the records and evidences bearing upon this point, and it would be presumption on my part to say one word about it. There is only one thing that I ask, and it is expressed in few words: Pass your sentence.

For six weary months I have been a prisoner; for six months my name has been in the mouth of every one; by thousands I am considered a monster of cruelty, a wretch that ought not to pollute the earth any longer. Truly, when I pass in my mind over the testimony given, I sometimes almost doubt my own existence. I doubt that I am the Captain Wirz spoken of. I am inclined to call on the mountains to fall upon and bury me and my shame. But oh, sir, while I wring my hands in mute and hopeless dispair, there speaks a small but unmistakable voice within me that says: Console thyself, thou knowest thy innocence. Fear not; if men hold thee guilty, God does not, and a new life will pervade your being. Such has been the state of my mind for weeks and months, and no punishment that human ingenuity can inflict could increases my distress.

GIVE ME LIBERTY OR GIVE ME DEATH

The pangs of death are short, and therefore I humbly pray that you will pass your sentence without delay. Give me death or liberty. The one I do not fear; the other I crave. If you believe me guilty of the terrible charges that have been heaped upon me, deliver me to the executioner. If not guilty, in your estimation, restore me to liberty and life. A life such as I am now living is no life. I breathe, sleep, eat, but it is only the mechanical functions I perform, and nothing more. Whatever you decide I shall accept. If restored to liberty, I will thank and bless you for it.

The death warrant is read to Captain Henry Wirz at his execution

I would not convey the idea to your mind, Mr. President, that I court death. Life is sweet; however lowly or humble man's station may be, he clings to life. His soul is filled with awe when he contemplates the future, the unknown land which the judgment is before which he will have to give an account of his words, thought, and deeds. Well may I remember, too, that I have erred like all other human beings. But of those things for which I may perhaps suffer a violent death, I am not guilty; and God judge me. I have said all that I wished to say. Excuse my boldness in addressing you, but I could not help it. I cannot bear this suspense much longer. May God bless you, and be with you; your task is a great and fearful one. In life or death I shall pray for you, and for the prosperity of the country in which I have passed some of my happiest as well as darkest days.

Respectfully,

H. Wirz

On the eve of his execution, Wirz was offered a pardon if he agreed to testify that Jefferson Davis bore responsibility for the gruesome conditions and deaths at Andersonville. Claiming the charges were false, Wirz refused to lie in order to save his life. On November 10, 1865, before 250 spectators and soldiers, some of whom were chanting "Remember Andersonville," Wirz emerged from his cell into the prison courtyard and ascended the gallows' stairs, whereupon a black hood was placed over his head and a rope tied around his neck. Death by hanging is usually quick because the neck snaps once the trap door is sprung and the condemned falls. In Wirz's case, however, his neck did not break, and he slowly swung in agony while the noose strangled him. Poet Walt Whitman wrote the following about Andersonville: "There are deeds, crimes that may be forgiven, but this is not among them. It steeps its perpetrators in blackest, escapeless, endless damnation."

TETSUZO HIRASAKI
TO MISS BREED,
Poston, Arizona, February 19, 1943,
World War II

Four days after Pearl Harbor, the FBI detained 1,370 Japanese Americans who had been classified as "dangerous enemy aliens." Many West Coast residents, fearing future Japanese attacks, sent a number of influential leaders to pressure Washington into forcibly moving law-abiding American citizens of Japanese extraction away from large population centers. By mid-February 1942, President Franklin D. Roosevelt had signed Executive Order 9066, sending 120,000 people of Japanese ancestry, two-thirds of whom were American citizens, into internment camps. The War Relocation Authority set up detention centers in isolated parts of the West, including Arizona, California, Colorado, Idaho, Utah, and Wyoming. The order was rescinded in 1944, and the last camps closed in March 1946—seven months after Japan's surrender. The recipient of this letter, Clara Breed, was a librarian in San Diego who, despite the mass hysteria gripping the country, corresponded with many of her students whose families had been rounded up and separated from home, friends, and relatives.

Dear Miss Breed,

This is prodigal reporting. Things
have been popping rather fast lately.
A windstorm (dust), a cold spell, a rainstorm
and good news.

The duststorm came during the
third week of January and lasted
for three days. It was almost as [bad]
as the Christmas storm. Following
that on the morning of Jan. 20
we had the coldest morning
when the temp. dropped to 20°.
That whole day ice was on the
ground. It wasn't until the
next afternoon before it thawed.
Then on the 23rd it began to
rain. It poured cloudburst after
cloudburst for three days. [T]

Dear Miss Breed,

This is prodigal reporting. Things have been popping rather fast lately. A (dust) windstorm, a cold spell, a rainstorm, and good news.

The duststorm came during the third week of January and lasted for three days. It was almost as bad as the Christmas storm. Following that on the morning of Jan. 20 we had the coldest morning yet when the temp. dropped to 20°. That whole day ice was on the ground. It wasn't until the next afternoon before it thawed. Then on the 23rd it began to rain. It poured cloudburst after cloudburst for three days. The dust just turned into the stickiest mud I have ever seen. It was during the same storm that you had that bad blow in San Diego. From the pictures in the clippings it must have been quite a blow.

When the Army came here to Camp III to register the men under selective service and also to take volunteers for the Japanese American Combat Unit, it was the best piece of news we nisei have had in a long time. We nisei were despairing in ever becoming recognized. But now we have the chance to prove our loyalty, because after the evacuation, nisei were classed as aliens ineligible for military service.

I am proud to say that the San Diego group has the most volunteers than any other group in camp. All together in our block we have just about 15 volunteers including yours truly, which makes about the best record yet. We are going around Feb 23 (according to those "in the know") to Camp Douglas, Utah (near Salt Lake City) for induction that to Camp Shelby Mississippi (this much is official) for training. This is the bunch to be with because we are all volunteers and there won't be those slackers and pro-axis minded as there would be if the men were drafted. Yessirree all of us are itching to go.

I also received news that the men in internment are possibly slated for rehearings according to a friend of mine who visited the Lordsburg New Mexico Internment Camp, just recently. He said he talked to my father and that he was looking fine. Treatment of the interned men is very fine.

I have been writing to a number of people for affidavits as I want my father to be eligible for a rehearing and a possible parole so that he can come to Poston to be with Yaeko. While I'm gone.

So—if everything goes well I'll be writing to you from an Army Camp instead of a relocation center.

On a plaque at Tetsuzo Hirasaki's relocation center in Poston is written, "May it serve as a constant reminder of our past so that Americans in the future will never again be denied their constitutional rights and may the remembrance of that experience serve to advance the evolution of the human spirit. . . ." Despite fears of Japanese sabotage and espionage, only ten people were convicted of spying for Japan during the entire war—all of them Caucasian.

An interesting note: The 100th Infantry Battalion of primarily Japanese-American National Guardsmen from Hawaii and the 442nd Regimental Combat Team comprising internment camp volunteers were highly decorated units that fought in eight major campaigns in North Africa and Europe, including Monte Cassino, Anzio, and Biffontaine. One of their most famous exploits was the rescue of the Texas National Guard's 1st Battalion, 141st Infantry Regiment (the "Lost Battalion"), in which 800 casualties were sustained in order to rescue 211 Texans. The units received 20 Medals of Honor.

Love and War

MAJOR SULLIVAN BALLOU
TO HIS WIFE, SARAH,
Camp Clark, Washington, D.C., July 14, 1861,
Civil War

Ballou joined the 2nd Regiment, Rhode Island Volunteers in the spring of 1861 when he was 32 years old. A successful lawyer, ardent Republican, and former speaker of the Rhode Island House of Representatives, Ballou and his 25-year-old wife, Sarah, had two young children, Edgar and Willie. On June 19, with less than a month's training, he and his men departed Providence for Washington, D.C. President Lincoln reviewed his brigade five days later, and on June 27, he and the first lady visited Camp Clark, where Ballou was stationed. On July 14, in the first of two letters he wrote to Sarah that day, Ballou stated his intention that she visit him at camp. But by nightfall, he suspected that he would soon be sent into action. He sat down to write her the following extraordinary letter.

SULLIVAN BALLOU,
MAJOR 2D REG'T,
R. I. VOLS.
DIED JULY 29, 1861,
AGED 32 YEARS.

―――――

"I WAIT FOR YOU THERE.
COME TO ME AND LEAD
THITHER MY CHILDREN."

BALLOU.

My very dear Sarah:

The indications are very strong that we shall move in a few days—perhaps tomorrow. Lest I should not be able to write you again, I feel impelled to write lines that may fall under your eye when I shall be no more.

Our movement may be one of a few days duration and full of pleasure—and it may be one of severe conflict and death to me. Not my will, but thine O God, be done. If it is necessary that I should fall on the battlefield for my country, I am ready. I have no misgivings about, or lack of confidence in, the cause in which I am engaged, and my courage does not halt or falter. I know how strongly American Civilization now leans upon the triumph of the Government, and how great a debt we owe to those who went before us through the blood and suffering of the Revolution. And I am willing—perfectly willing—to lay down all my joys in this life, to help maintain this Government, and to pay that debt.

But, my dear wife, when I know that with my own joys I lay down nearly all of yours, and replace them in this life with cares and sorrows—when, after having eaten for long years the bitter fruit of orphanage myself, I must offer it as their only sustenance to my dear little children—is it weak or dishonorable, while the banner of my purpose floats calmly and proudly in the breeze, that my unbounded love for you, my darling wife and children, should struggle in fierce, though useless, contest with my love of country?

I cannot describe to you my feelings on this calm summer night, when two thousand men are sleeping around me, many of them enjoying the last, perhaps, before that of death—and I, suspicious that Death is creeping behind me with his fatal dart, am communing with God, my country, and thee.

I have sought most closely and diligently, and often in my breast, for a wrong motive in thus hazarding the happiness of those I loved and I could not find one. A pure love of my country and of the principles I

. . . and I, suspicious that Death is creeping behind me with his fatal dart, am communing with God, my country, and thee. . . . Sarah, my love for you is deathless, it seems to bind me to you with mighty cables that nothing but Omnipotence could break. . . .

have often advocated before the people and "the name of honor that I love love more than I fear death" have called upon me, and I have obeyed.

Sarah, my love for you is deathless, it seems to bind me to you with mighty cables that nothing but Omnipotence could break; and yet my love of Country comes over me like a strong wind and bears me irresistibly on with all these chains to the battlefield.

The memories of the blissful moments I have spent with you come creeping over me, and I feel most gratified to God and to you that I have enjoyed them so long. And hard it is for me to give them up and burn to ashes the hopes of future years, when God willing, we might still have lived and loved together and seen our sons grow up to honorable manhood around us. I have, I know, but few and small claims upon Divine

Providence, but something whispers to me—perhaps it is the wafted prayer of my little Edgar—that I shall return to my loved ones unharmed. If I do not, my dear Sarah, never forget how much I love you, and when my last breath escapes me on the battlefield, it will whisper your name.

Forgive my many faults, and the many pains I have caused you. How thoughtless and foolish I have oftentimes been! How gladly would I wash out with my tears every little spot upon your happiness, and struggle with all the misfortune of this world, to shield you and my children from harm. But I cannot. I must watch you from the spirit land and hover near you, while you buffet the storms with your precious little freight, and wait with sad patience till we meet to part no more.

But, O Sarah! If the dead can come back to this earth and flit unseen around those they loved, I shall always be near you; in the garish day and in the darkest night—amidst your happiest scenes and gloomiest hours—always, always; and if there be a soft breeze upon your cheek, it shall be my breath; or the cool air fans your throbbing temple, it shall be my spirit passing by.

Sarah, do not mourn me dead; think I am gone and wait for thee, for we shall meet again.

As for my little boys, they will grow as I have done, and never know a father's love and care. Little Willie is too young to remember me long, and my blue-eyed Edgar will keep my frolics with him among the dimmest memories of his childhood. Sarah, I have unlimited confidence in your maternal care and your development of their characters. Tell my two mothers his and hers I call God's blessing upon them. O Sarah, I wait for you there! Come to me, and lead thither my children.

Sullivan

On Tuesday, July 16, 1861, Ballou and 35,000 soldiers marched out of Washington and crossed into Virginia as the 2nd New

Hampshire band contemptuously played "Dixie." By the second day, Ballou's unit had camped in a beautiful meadow, where he wrote Sarah of the enemy's retreat before their arrival. In what was later known as the First Battle of Bull Run, Ballou was ordered to lead two divisions in an attempt to outflank the Confederates at Sudley Ford, and in the early morning hours of July 21, he assembled his troops. The shooting had barely begun when a Confederate cannonball struck and killed Ballou's horse and crushed his leg. Sent back to a field hospital, doctors were forced to amputate, and Ballou was later captured. He died of his wounds on July 29. When his personal effects were shipped back home to Sarah, this magnificent letter was discovered in a trunk. It had never been sent, and the original has since disappeared.

PRIVATE FRANCIS CHRISTIANCE TO HIS WIFE,

Alexandra Heights, October 7, 1861,

Civil War

C ivil War desertions were an ongoing, complex issue for both the Union and Confederate armies. By late 1862, after only one and a half years of war, the Union provost marshal announced that more than 100,000 men had deserted their posts, with nearly 45,000 deserters in New York State alone. The problem was so serious in the South that in August 1863, President Jefferson Davis offered amnesty to all those who were absent without leave. The reasons for desertion were many, and not always connected with cowardly retreat in the heat of battle. Payment was poor and often very late, morale was low due to the terrible conditions in both armies, sick leave and furlough passes were often abused, and many of the families that soldiers left behind encountered considerable economic hardship. Another factor contributing to the high rate of desertion was the demoralizing effect of soldiers killing soldiers who until recently had shared a common citizenship.

One deserter, a soldier named Henry Andrews, had his case brought before President Abraham Lincoln. On January 7, 1864, Lincoln wrote, "The case of Andrews is really a very bad one, as

I this day received an issue of the <u>Star and Times</u> containing the following paragraphs which no doubt overwhelmed me as much as it certainly must have done you....

appears by the record already before me. Yet before receiving this, I had ordered his punishment commuted to imprisonment at hard labor and had so telegraphed. I did this, not on any merit in the case, but because I am trying to evade the butchering business lately." A Union soldier wrote the following letter home.

Dear Wife,

I this day received an issue of the Star and Times *containing the following paragraphs which no doubt overwhelmed me as much as it certainly must have done you.* "To be shot: Francis Christaince deserter from the ranks of Capt. Truax'es Company, one which we have known for a long time was sentenced to be shot and perhaps met his faith at noon to-day. We have not given this fact publicity before, we did hope for and do not yet despair of a reprieve for the misguided soldier though the fact that this terrible punishment is meted for a second offense seems to abide it:—"

I simply deny in to each and every specification contained in the above.

1st. I am not shot.

2nd. I am not sentenced to be shot.

3rd. There has not been here the slightest supposition among the men or myself that I was to be shot.

4th. I never deserted from Capt. Truax'es Company nor have I ever been tried for any charge for desertion. From whence these false assertions could have originated I cannot surmise. But if he has feeling for a kind and loving wife, a household of children, not to say of the grief that fills your heart at this report, he certainly would not be humanity to contradict it.

This afternoon Col. Jackson has received a letter requesting the transmission of my dead body to my wife, my feeling may better be imagined than described. The editor of the Star certainly should bare a great deal of the blame for publishing a rumor leaving a whole family on the foundation of what must have been a mere rumor, but this is not the first nor I suppose the last kindness we will receive from those we left behind.

Truly your loving and yet living husband,

Francis Christiance

LEON [LAST NAME WITHHELD] TO HIS FIANCÉE,

Korea, June 15, 1952,

Korean War

The vast and extreme magnitude of the tragedy called war is most often expressed and comprehended in terms of its physical cost and destruction of property and people. But there is another cost that in some respects is even more destructive—the psychological. It is difficult, if not impossible, to find an event more devastating to the morale of a combatant than the receipt of a Dear John letter.

On June 14, 1952, a 19-year-old artillery gunner named Leon, serving with the 34th Field Artillery Battalion of the 25th Infantry Division, received a Dear John letter from his fiancée. His response, written the next day, was not just a farewell to his girl, but a farewell to his life. On June 17, he charged a Chinese Communist machine-gun emplacement on his own and was killed.

You tried to "let me down easy." Well, if it's any consolation to you, you did it about as well as a thing like that can be done. But, then, we wouldn't have wanted it to have been too easy, would we?

Dear Babe,

I just received your last letter in this morning's mail. I held it in my hand for a minute while a little voice in the back of my head whispered, "This is it. This is the one." Oh yeah, I knew it was coming. I could tell from the tone of your last few letters. Have you forgotten how well we know each other?

You tried to "let me down easy." Well, if it's any consolation to you, you did it about as well as a thing like that can be done. But, then, we wouldn't have wanted it to have been too easy, would we?

You ask me if I understand. I do. I never said I was the greatest guy on earth; you did. I just agreed with you: but, to be fair, we didn't mention any other places. You didn't mention what planet you were going to live on, either; this, or his. Anyway, he's there. I'm here.

"Be careful," you tell me. "Take care." I almost laughed out loud. We wouldn't want to see me hurt, would we? There's no need to worry *about me. I'll be all right. I swear it. You have other things to think about now. Hopes to hope. Wishes to wish. Dreams to dream. A life to live; and, I wish you the best of all there is.*

Now? Now I will do what I have no choice but to do. But how? Do I say something brilliant like "may all your troubles be little ones"? Or do I treat this like a tennis match? "I did my best; it just wasn't good enough, and the best man won." How's that?

How about "If you ever need a friend"?

That presumes a future. There are 500,000 N. Koreans and Chinese on the other side of that hill bound and determined to make sure I don't have a future. Over here where your past is your last breath, your present is this breath, and your future is your next breath, you don't make too many promises. Which leaves me <u>what</u>?

Goodbye
Leon

CAPTAIN JOHN PAUL JONES TO COUNTESS SELKIRK,

on board the <u>Ranger,</u> Brest, France, May 8, 1778,

American Revolution

Considered by historians to be the "father" of the U.S. Navy, John Paul Jones was born in Scotland in 1747. He immigrated to America at age 12, and by 1775, he had been commissioned a first lieutenant aboard the frigate *Alfred*. He later became her captain and successfully terrorized the British merchant fleet by destroying ships and boldly raiding fisheries.

Britain experienced heavy losses from the attacks of 10,000 Americans sailing in privateers. Privateers were, in effect, legalized pirate ships. Each captain carried documents known as letters of marque that were authorized by the Continental Congress as well as the individual states. They both sanctioned the raiding of British merchant vessels and authorized the privateers to keep a percentage of the cargo they captured. Privateers were responsible for the seizure or destruction of 2,000 ships, the capture of 12,000 men, and the loss of £18 million worth of goods. Indeed, many of the colonial navy's first sailors joined in order to line their pockets with plunder.

Jones received a commission signed by John Hancock in 1777 to command the sloop of war *Ranger*—one of the first ships to fly the Stars and Stripes. After sailing from Portsmouth, New Hampshire, on November 1, 1777, Jones raided Whitehaven in northern England the following April. He then headed to nearby St. Mary's Isle in his native Scotland with the intention of kidnapping the earl of Selkirk and holding him hostage in exchange for American prisoners of war. Leading a small shore party, Jones marched up to the Selkirk mansion, where he discovered that the earl was absent. Before returning on board, he allowed his disgruntled men, under the strictest orders, to take just the Selkirk family silver as booty. Countess Selkirk, in the house with her son, several daughters, and a few guests and staff, first thought the sailors were pirates, but retained her composure while allowing them to make off with the silver. Before they left, she even had the temerity to ask for a receipt for the expensive service. The next day, Jones and his men captured the HMS *Drake,* the first victory of an American warship over the enemy, and towed her to the port of Brest, France. He then wrote and sent off the following remarkably naive and quite flirtatious letter to the countess.

★

Madam:

It cannot be too much lamented that in the profession of Arms, the Officer of fine feelings, and of real Sensibility, should be under the necessity of winking at any action of Persons under his command, which his Heart cannot approve:—but the reflection is doubly severe when he finds himself Obliged, in appearance, to countenance such Action by his Authority.

This hard case was mine when on the 23rd of April last I landed on St. Mary's Isle. Knowing Lord Selkirk's intrest with his King, and esteeming as I do *his private Character; I wished to make him the happy Instrument of alleviating the horrors of hopeless captivity, when the brave are overpowered and made Prisoners of War.*

It was perhaps fortunate for you Madam that he was from home; for it was my intention to have taken him on board the Ranger, *and to have detained him till thro' his means, a general and fair Exchange of Prisoners, as well in Europe as in America had been effected.*

When I was informed by some Men whom I met at landing, that his Lordship was absent; I walked back to my Boat determining to leave the Island: by the way, however, some Officers who were with me could not forbear expressing their discontent; observing that in America no delicacy was shown by the English; who took away all sorts of movable Property, setting Fire not only to Towns and to Houses of the rich without distinction; but not even sparing the wretched hamlets and Milch Cows of the poor and helpless at the approach of an inclement Winter. That party had been with me, as Volunteers, the same morning at White Haven; some complaisance therefore was their due. I had but a moment to think how I might gratify them, and at the same time do your Ladyship the least Injury. I charged the Two Officers to permit none of the Seamen to enter the House, or to hurt anything about it—To treat you, Madam, with the utmost Respect—to accept of the plate which was offered—and to come away without making a search or demanding anything else.

I am induced to believe that I was punctually Obeyed; since I am informed that the plate which they brought away is far short of the Inventory which accompanied it. I have gratified my Men; and when the plate is sold, I shall become the Purchaser, and I will gratify my own feelings by restoring it to you, by such conveyance as you shall be pleased to direct.

Had the Earl been on board the Ranger *the following Evening he would have seen the awful Pomp and dreadful Carnage of a Sea Engagement, both affording ample subject for the Pencil, as well as melancholy reflection for the contemplative mind. Humanity starts back from such scenes of horror, and cannot but execrate the vile Promoters of this detested War.*

    For They, *t'was* THEY *unsheath'd the ruthless blade,*
    And Heav'n shall ask the Havock it has made.

    The British Ship of War, Drake, *mounting 20 guns, with more than her full complement of Officers and Men, besides a number of Volunteers, came out from Carrickfergus, in order to attack and take the American Continental Ship of War,* Ranger, *of 18 guns and short of her complement of Officers and Men. The Ships met, and the advantage was disputed with great fortitude on each side for an Hour and Five minutes, when the gallant Commander of the* Drake *fell, and Victory declared in favor of the* Ranger. *His amiable Lieutenant lay mortally wounded besides near forty of the inferior officers and crew killed and wounded. A melancholy demonstration of the uncertainty of human prospects, and of the sad reverse of fortune which an hour can produce. I buried them in a spacious grave, with the Honors due to the memory of the brave.*

    Tho' I have drawn my Sword in the present generous Struggle for the rights of Men; yet I am not in Arms as an American, nor am I in pursuit of Riches. My Fortune is liberal enough, having no Wife nor Family, and having lived long enough to know that Riches cannot ensure Happiness. I profess myself a Citizen of the World, totally unfettered by the little mean distinctions of Climate or of Country, which diminish the benevolence of the Heart and set bounds to Philanthropy. Before this War began I had at an early time of Life, withdrawn from the Sea service, in favor of "calm contemplation and Poetic ease." I have sacrificed not only my favorite scheme of Life, but the softer Affections of the Heart *and my prospects of Domestic Happiness:—And I am ready to sacrifice Life also with cheerfulness—if that forfeiture could restore Peace and Goodwill among mankind.*

As the feelings of your gentle Bosom cannot but be congenial with mine—let me entreat you Madam to use your soft persuasive Arts with your Husband to endeavor to stop this Cruel and destructive War, in which Britain can never succeed. Heaven can never countenance the barbarous and unmanly Practices of the Britons in America, which Savages would Blush at; and which if not discontinued will soon be retaliated in Britain by a justly enraged People.—Should you fail in this, (for I am persuaded you will attempt it; and who can resist the power of such an Advocate?) Your endeavours to effect a general Exchange of Prisoners, will be an Act of Humanity, which will afford you Golden feelings on a Death bed.

I hope this cruel contest will soon be closed, but should it continue, I wage no War with the Fair. I acknowledge their Power, and bend before it with profound Submission; let not therefore the Amiable Countess of Selkirk regard me as an Enemy. I am ambitious of her esteem and Friendship, and would do anything consistent with my duty to merit it.

The honor of a Line from your hand in Answer to this will lay me under a very singular Obligation; and if I can render you any acceptable service in France or elsewhere, I hope you see into my character so far as to command me without the least grain of reserve.

I wish to know exactly the behavior of my People, as I determine to punish them if they have exceeded their Liberty.

I have the Honor to be with much Esteem and with profound Respect,

Madam,

Your most Obedient and most humble Servant

J^{NO} P. JONES

Jones was very proud of his letter to the countess; so proud, in fact, that to ensure its safe delivery, he sent her three separate holograph originals by different conveyances. Other copies were sent to diplomats Benjamin Franklin and Arthur Lee in Paris, and a copy was included in his *Memoire* to French king Louis XVI. Jones made good on his promise to return the Selkirk's silver, and at the war's conclusion, at great trouble and expense, he sent it back to the earl and countess. Best remembered for his famous reply when asked to surrender during the battle between the *Bonhomme Richard* and the British *Serapis,* "I have not yet begun to fight," he might well have added, "Nor have I yet begun to write!"

GENERAL DWIGHT D. EISENHOWER
TO HIS WIFE, MAMIE,

October 30, 1942,

World War II

A West Point graduate in 1915, Eisenhower rose through the ranks of the army over the next 25 years to become a brigadier general in 1941. Up to that point he had excelled as a staff officer. World War II changed his career path. In the fall of 1942, then a lieutenant general, Eisenhower was given his first major test as a commander. His assignment, to oversee the Allied invasion of North Africa, code-named Operation Torch, was set to begin in early November 1942. The invasion was ordered despite the lukewarm support of Churchill and F. D. R.'s military advisers, in part because of a promise to Soviet premier Josef Stalin to divert Axis resources and reduce pressure on the Russian front. F. D. R. also had domestic considerations: He wanted to impress upon his countrymen that America was fully committed to the vigilant pursuit and successful outcome of the war against Germany and Italy in the west and Japan in the east. Victory in North Africa was achieved in May 1943, by which time Eisenhower had been promoted to full general. Upon his return from the Teheran Conference in December 1943, F. D. R., well pleased with Eisenhower's management of Operation

Dwight D. Eisenhower reads a letter as Mamie looks on

Torch, told him, "Well, Ike, you are going to command Overlord," the Allied invasion of Europe in June 1944. Overlord became Eisenhower's greatest military accomplishment—the largest invasion in history lead by an officer who had never held a combat command. Less than two weeks before Operation Torch was to begin, Eisenhower wrote this moving birthday letter to Mamie, his wife of 26 years.

★

By the time you read this your newspapers will probably tell you where I am and you will understand why your birthday letter had to be written some time in advance. You will also realize that I have been busy, very busy, and any lapse in the arrival of letters will be explained to you. Knowing that all this will be plain to you by the time you read this I am not compelled to violate rules of secrecy and censorship in order to tell you what I am planning to do.

I hope you won't be disturbed or worried. War inevitably carries its risks to life and limb—but the chances, in my case, are all in my favor, a fact which you must always remember. Moreover—even if the worst should happen to me, please don't be too upset. In my 31 years as a soldier I've been exposed to few of the risks that most have encountered. If I had been in the Theatre of Operations in World War I, I might easily have long since been gone. And, while I don't mean to be fatalistic or too philosophical—I truly feel that what the U.S. and the world are facing today is so much bigger than any one of us can even comprehend, that personal sacrifice and loss must not be allowed to overwhelm any of us.

Anyway, on the day you open this letter you'll be 46. I'd like to be there to help you celebrate, and to kiss you 46 times (multiplied by any number you care to pick). I imagine Ruth will have some little party for you, or maybe Helen and Milton will try to get hold of you. In any event, I will be with you in thought, and entirely aside from the usual congratulations and felicitations, I will be thinking with the deepest gratitude of the many happy hours and years you've given me. I'm quite aware of the fact that I'm not always easy to live with—that frequently I'm irascible and even mean—and my gratitude is even greater when I realize how often you've put up with me in spite of such traits.

The crowning thing you've given me is our son—he has been so wonderful, unquestionably because he's so much you—that I find I live in him so very often. Your love and our son have been my greatest gifts from life, and on your birthday I wish that my powers of expression were such as to make you understand that thoroughly—clearly and for always. I've never wanted any other wife—you're mine, and for that reason I've been luckier than any other man.

I feel this war is so big—so vast—that my mind completely refuses to visualize anything beyond its possible end. But I do hope that all through it I do my duty so well, so efficiently, that regardless of what may happen to me, you and John can always be proud that we three are one family. I do not seek rank—I don't even seek acclaim, because it is easily possible that a commander can receive credit (and blame) for which he is in no way responsible. But, if my own conscience tells me I've done my duty—I will always come back to you in the certainty that you'd understand any fall from the high places, and that my place in your heart would be as big as ever.

Again—love and kisses on your birthday!

Dwight D. Eisenhower

AN UNKNOWN SOLDIER TO HATTIE,

February 9, 1864,

Civil War

An unknown Union lieutenant from the 11th New York Battery placed a "lonely hearts" advertisement in the *Waverly Advocate*, a New York newspaper. A woman named Hattie wrote to him and he promptly responded to the "charming little epistle" he had received. One cannot help but admire this hopeful suitor who candidly confesses that he exaggerated certain facts about himself and proceeds to set things right—and later cannily gives her the opportunity to confess that she may have embellished a bit as well. The conclusion of the letter has been lost, leaving us to use our imagination to complete the interrupted thought and hope that even if they did not meet and marry, at least he survived.

Dear Hattie

Pardon the affectionate familiarity but you know its all in fun. Your charming little epistle has just reached me, and I do myself the honor to answer it immediately, thus complying with your request to write soon.

Before proceeding farther truth and candor compel me to acknowledge that a little desception was used in the advertisement in the "Waverly."

Before proceeding farther truth and candor compel me to acknowledge that a little desception was used in the advertisement in the "Waverly." *In other words my true description differs materially from the one therein set forth, and may not please you as well as the one "fancy painted," but I thought it was all for fun, therefore funningly gave a fictitious description as well as cognomen. Be it known unto you then, this individual is twenty-nine years of age, five feet and eleven inches high, dark blue eyes, brown hair, and light (ruddy) complexion. There you have it. How do you like the descripion? Me thinks I hear you answer. I dont like it so well as the advertised description. Well! I'll admit it is not quite so fascinating to a young lady as the fictitious one, but it is a fixed fact, "like the laws of the Medes and Persians," which altereth not. But enough of that topic for the present! The next thing, will undoubtedly be something else.*

It is said, that a person's writing is indication of their character, if so, judging from your letter, I take you to be of one that class know as "romps"—a class by the way, which I rather admire. Commend me to a girl who has life and animation enough to enjoy the harmless pleasures of this beautiful world, in preference to your "Miss Prim," who

would not dare to laugh in louder tones than a whimpering sentimen-
tal snicker, for fear of overstepping the bounds of etiquette.

No indeed! None of your "Miss Prims" for me. I love the gaily ringing
laugh of true and gladsome hearts. Of course I would not have a young
lady act in an imbecoming or unladylike manner, but I believe in giving
free scope to thou joyous feelings, implanted in the soul by a wise and
kind "creator" to cheer us through life's checkered pathway looking over
the -----. Could you have been within hearing distance when I read you
letter, you would have heard a laugh that made this old tent ring, espe-
cially when I came to the sentence, "Sing Heigh Ho for a husband"—I
just laid back in my chair + roared—thats decidedly rich! I don't sup-
pose that you entertain thoughts of Matrimony. Who ever knows a
young lady that did? but if so you have my best wishes that your song
may be speedily answered, on condition, that I have an invitation to the
wedding.

You say you have returned from boarding school for a few months
on account of delicate health. No doubt it is great treat for you, to again
be, with the loved ones at home. I do not wonder at your hating board-
ing school, for as generally conducted they are about as injurious to girls
health, as beneficial to her education. I firmly believe that hundreds of
girls die annually from the pernicious effects of boarding school train-
ing. I presume the description given of yourself is partly fictitious. I
aught not to doubt a lady word, but am aware that in correspondence
of this character a great deal of description is generally used.

I promised on the honor of a gentleman and soldier that I have thus
far given a true description of myself, it remains for me to add that I
was formerly a private, but am now a Lieut in Uncle Samuel's service
and that my true name is signed to this letter. Enclosed please find carte-
de-visites of your incognito, when you answer this which I hope you will
do without fail—be kind enough to give a correct description and
enclose a carte-de-visite, or Photograph, of your own sweet self.

The enclosed picture is not as good as it might be—the eyes are too light, the features however and general expression of the countenance are natural.

You ask for a description of "camp life," but I have written so much other stuff I will defer that until another time, suffice it to say the "Blue Jackets" are pretty comfortably situated—for soldiers—in winter quarters, where they will probably remain until the time comes for then sally forth to me—the nailorous "grey back" in battle array. When that time shall

The letter ends abruptly and without a signature.

Pride and Prejudice

CAPTAIN PHILIP TROUNSTINE
TO MAJOR C. S. HAYES,

Moscow, Tennessee, March 3, 1863,

Civil War

The following letter is a response to Union general Ulysses S. Grant's astonishing and infamous General Order No. 11 issued on December 17, 1862: "The Jews, as a class violating every regulation of trade established by the Treasury Department and also department orders, are hereby expelled from the department [i.e., the Union army of occupation's designation for Kentucky, Tennessee, and Mississippi] within 24 hours from the receipt of this order. Post commanders will see to it that all of this class of people be furnished passes and required to leave, and any one returning after such notification will be arrested and held in confinement until an opportunity occurs of sending them out as prisoners, unless furnished with permit from headquarters. No passes will be given these people to visit headquarters for the purpose of making personal applications of trade permits."

Like so many other examples of prejudice against Jews, Grant's order was rooted in economics. The North had captured large stocks of cotton and other goods. As both the Treasury Department and the Army were charged with distributing this cache, the responsibility

General Ulysses S. Grant

fell to Grant, who commanded of the Department of the Tennessee. High cotton prices in the North prompted some individuals without permits to bribe Union officers so they could buy Southern cotton and cash in on large profits. Grant was beside himself with anger when his own father visited him to apply for permits on behalf of a number of merchants from Cincinnati, some of whom were Jewish.

Grant's unfavorable opinion of Jews was shared by Union army commander Henry Halleck. By November 1862, Grant had decreed that "no Jews are to be permitted to travel on the railroad southward from any point" and that the requisite trade permits would not be issued. He remained convinced that the black market in cotton was constituted "mostly by Jews and other unprincipled traders" and issued General Order No. 11 when illegal trading by overwhelmingly non-Jewish speculators continued. In some cases, well-established Southern Jewish families (and Union army veterans) were forced to leave their homes in 24 hours. President Lincoln received telegrams, letters, petitions, and several delegations of citizens and politicians who objected to Grant's outrageous conduct. In early January, shortly after the Emancipation Proclamation went into effect, Lincoln instructed Halleck to have Grant revoke his order, which he did three days later. In the following letter a Jewish officer offers his resignation to protest General Grant's order.

Major!

I respectfully address you, on the subject of tendering you with this, my resignation of the commission I now hold, as Captain of Company "B" 5th Regt. Ohio Volunteer Cavalry. The reasons for offering the above, are few, and I shall therefore try to be as concise as possible in presenting them to your consideration. You are perhaps well aware of my having been, whether fortunately or unfortunately born of Jewish parents; my future must of course decide which; you will therefore bear with me, Major, when I say that not alone my feelings, but the sense of Religious duty, I owe to the religion of my Forefathers, were both deeply hurt and wounded in consequence of the late order of General Grant issued December 17th 1862, in which all persons of collateral religious faith with my own, were ordered to leave this Department. I do not wish to argue the question of Order No. 11 being either right or wrong, nor would I, if even I dared to. But I cannot help feeling, that as I owe filial affection to my parents, Devotion to my Religion, and a deep regard for the opinion of my friends and feeling that I can no longer bear the Taunts and malice of those to whom my religious opinions are known, brought on by the effect that that order has instilled into their minds. I herewith respectfully tender you my immediate and unconditional resignation.

I certify upon honor that I have no property belonging to the Government of the United States in my possession. I was last paid by paymaster Major Jordan to include August 31st 1862.

I have the honor to be, Major,
Very respectfully Your Obedient Servant
Philip Troustine

General Order No. 11 resurfaced as an issue during the presidential campaign of 1868 when Grant was chosen over President Andrew Johnson as the Republican candidate. Grant wrote an old friend, Isaac Morris: "There were many other persons within my lines equally bad with the worst of them, but the difference was that the Jews could pass with impunity from one army to the other, and gold in violation of order, was being smuggled through the lines. . . . The order was issued and sent without any reflection and without thinking of the Jews as a sect or race to themselves, but simply as persons who had successfully . . . violated an order, which greatly inured to the help of the rebels. . . . I have no prejudice against sect or race, but want each individual to be judged by his own merit. General Order No. 11 does not sustain that statement, I admit, but then I do not sustain that order. It never would have been issued if it had not been telegraphed the moment it was penned and without reflection."

PRIVATE CANUTE FRANKSON
TO A FRIEND,
Albacete, Spain, July 6, 1937,
Spanish Civil War

Think of Pablo Picasso's monumental painting depicting the destruction of Guernica, Spain. Think of Ernest Hemingway's *For Whom the Bell Tolls*. Think of George Orwell's *Homage to Catalonia*, and then think of an American autoworker named Canute Frankson, one of 80 African-Americans who fought in the Abraham Lincoln Brigade during the Spanish civil war. Until he fell in battle, another African-American from Chicago, Oliver Law, was a commander in the Lincoln Brigade—the first officer of his race to lead a fully integrated American military unit. The brigade's 2,800 volunteers, along with 40,000 others from 52 countries, were determined to defend a fledgling Spanish Republic against General Francisco Franco's fascist armed forces and his supporters, Adolf Hitler and Benito Mussolini.

Spain became a military and political dress rehearsal that tested the world's resolve against fascism. Emboldened by the tepid response to events in Spain and Czechoslovakia, and the nonaggression pact with Russia, Hitler had every reason to feel confident of German victory when his army crossed the Polish border on

Propoganda poster from the Spanish Civil War

September 1, 1939, raising the curtain on the first act of the Second
World War.

★

My Dear Friend:

*I'm sure that by this time you are still waiting for a detailed expla-
nation of what has this international struggle to do with my being here.
Since this is a war between whites who for centuries have held us in
slavery, and have heaped every kind of insult and abuse upon us, segre-
gated and jim-crowed us; why I, a Negro who has fought through these
years for the rights of my people, am here in Spain today?*

*Because we are no longer an isolated minority group fighting hope-
lessly against an immense giant. Because, my dear, we have joined with,
and become an active part of, a great progressive force, on whose shoulders rests the responsibility of saving human civilization from the
planned destruction of a small group of degenerates gone mad in their
lust for power. Because if we crush Fascism here we'll save our people in
America, and in other parts of the world from the vicious persecution,
wholesale imprisonment, and slaughter which the Jewish people suffered and are suffering under Hitler's Fascist heels.*

*All we have to do is to think of the lynching of our people. We can
but look back at the pages of American history stained with the blood
of Negroes; stink with the burning bodies of our people hanging from
trees; bitter with the groans of our tortured loved ones from whose living
bodies ears, fingers, toes have been cut for souvenirs—living bodies into
which red-hot pokers have been thrust. All because of a hate created in
the minds of men and women by their masters who keep us all under
their heels while they suck our blood, while they live in their bed of ease
by exploiting us.*

*But these people who howl like hungry wolves for our blood, must
we hate them? Must we keep the flame which these masters kindled*

constantly fed? Are these men and women responsible for the programs of their masters, and the conditions which force them to such degraded depths? I think not. They are tools in the hands of unscrupulous masters. These same people are as hungry as we are. They live in dives and wear rags the same as we do. They, too, are robbed by the masters, and their faces kept down in the filth of a decayed system. They are our fellow men. Soon, and very soon, they and we will understand. Soon, many Angelo Herndons will rise from among them, and from among us, and will lead us both against those who live by the stench of our burnt flesh. We will crush them. We will build us a new society—a society of peace and plenty. There will be no color line, no jim-crow trains, no lynching. That is why, my dear, I'm here in Spain.

Canute

By the time the Spanish civil war ended in 1939, about 1,000 fighters in the Abraham Lincoln Brigade had perished; and because many volunteers were Communists, the survivors faced blacklisting and persecution in the years following their return to the States. Nearly 60 years later, the Spanish government bestowed honorary citizenship on all brigade members. The great American poet Langston Hughes remarked, "Before that time, the leading ambassadors of the Negro people in Europe were jazz-band musicians, concert artists, dancers, or other performers. But these Negroes in Spain were fighters—voluntary fighters—which is where history turned another page."

1ST LIEUTENANT KEVIN KELLEY
TO THE EDITOR OF <u>STARS AND STRIPES,</u>

Darmstadt, Germany, September 29, 2001,

Operation Enduring Freedom

*saw a terrorist today. He was not carrying a gun or knife, nor did he
have explosives taped around his body. He was just an average looking Middle Eastern man, walking with his wife and child. They
were also terrorists. This is the legacy of the Sept. 11 attacks.*

*Intellectually, we can all understand and appreciate President
Bush's pleas to not lump all followers of Islam into that group of extrem-
ists we now know as our enemy. We know that the vast majority of
Middle Easterners are peaceful people who want nothing to do with
extremist activity. But that does not change the end result of the Sept.
11 attacks. From now on, every American, save a few truly enlightened
and trusting (or naive) souls, will look upon Islam as the religion of terror, and Middle Easterners as the agents of terror.*

*There will be a fundamental change concerning how Middle
Easterners (or those who look even remotely so) are treated within the
United States and much of Europe. Expect prejudice and paranoia to be
the rule. The prejudice will on occasion manifest itself as a hate crime,
but more often and likely as subtle discrimination. Hiring practices,
admission to universities and training centers, immigration policies—all*

these will certainly be affected. As for paranoia, the next time readers are in an airport and see someone of Middle Eastern descent, what will be the very first thought that comes to mind?

The terrorists have brought tragedy to our nation, but they have failed their own people. In war, innocents bear the heaviest burden. This war will not be any different. The many will pay the price for the actions of the few. God bless America.

1st Lt. Kevin Kelley
Darmstadt, Germany

The issues that Kelley's sad letter raises are profound and strike at the core of prejudice and war. The enemy, whether foreign or domestic, loses its face and personality. Individuality is obliterated, and the adversary is defined solely by his wealth, religion, color, ethnicity, politics, or nationality. He has been simplified and generalized in order to magnify his danger and to rally public opinion as quickly and easily as possible. This is how fear, anger, and intolerance are fostered during crises, and these are the methods that repressive regimes rely upon to mobilize their citizenry into armed action against another country.

Last Letters Home

WILLIAM B. TRAVIS
TO THE PEOPLE OF TEXAS,

The Alamo, February 24, 1836,

The Texan Revolution

The struggle for Texan independence is most dramatically recalled in the Battle of the Alamo. Less than 200 Texan and Tejano volunteers (the terms commonly used at the time to describe residents from Texas), along with legendary leaders William Travis, Davy Crockett, and Jim Bowie, held off a 13-day siege by a 4,000-man Mexican army under General Santa Anna. The bloody fighting in the compound of the former Spanish mission on the morning of March 6, 1836, was over in an hour. Six hundred Mexican soldiers lay dead or wounded, and all of the Alamo's defenders were killed with the exception of about 20 women, children, and slaves. Documents suggest that Travis died early in the battle, but Bowie and Crockett's deaths remain a mystery. Some historians claim that Bowie and a few other volunteers survived and were later executed by Santa Anna. In any event, all the defenders' corpses were burned.

Santa Anna, who regularly underestimated the strength and will of the Texan revolutionaries, was defeated and captured six weeks later by Sam Houston at the Battle of San Jacinto. Of

Battle of the Alamo by Pery Moran

debatable military value, the revolutionaries' heroic "last stand," memorialized in Colonel Sidney Sherman's words, "Remember the Alamo!" contributed to the Mexican defeat at San Jacinto. The Mexican army controlled the Alamo until May 1836, when they were ordered to destroy the fort. Some walls were torn down, but by June, Texan forces had entered San Antonio, and found the Mexicans gone.

Texan Independence led to its admission into the Union in 1845 and the Mexican War of 1846–1848. Mexico's final defeat gave the United States vast western territories, including New Mexico, Arizona, and California. Santa Anna died a pauper in Mexico City in 1876.

I shall <u>never</u> surrender or retreat. Then, I call on you in the name of Liberty, of patriotism, & every thing dear to the American character, to come to our aid, with all dispatch....

Fellow citizens & compatriots—

I am besieged, by a thousand or more of the Mexicans under Santa Anna—I have sustained a continual Bombardment & cannonade for 24 hours & have not lost a man—The enemy has demanded a surrender at discretion, otherwise, the garrison are to be put to the sword, if the fort is taken—I have answered the demand with a cannon shot, & our flag still waves proudly from the walls—I shall <u>never</u> surrender or retreat. Then, I call on you in the name of Liberty, of patriotism, & every thing dear to the American character, to come to our aid, with all dispatch—The enemy is receiving reinforcements daily & will no doubt increase to three or four thousand in four or five days. If this call is neglected, I am determined to sustain myself as long as possible & die like a soldier who never forgets what is due to his own honor & that of his country—

VICTORY OR DEATH

William Barret Travis

How was Travis's plea for assistance, so eloquently expressed in his letter, answered? The only documented display of support was the arrival of a few men from nearby Gonzales. A larger force under Colonel James Fannin at Goliad, about 100 miles away, could not help as they themselves were facing units of the Mexican army.

Divorced and a father of a 3-year-old son, Travis's last written message before his death was this short note, "Take care of my little boy. If the country should be saved, I may make for him a splendid fortune; but if the country be lost and I should perish, he will have nothing but the proud recollection that he is the son of a man who died for his country."

CONFEDERATE SOLDIER "L. B. F." TO JOHN H. VANNUYS,

Chaffin's Farm, Virginia,

after September 29, 1864,

Civil War

The brief note quoted below is an early example of a "dog tag," the military means of verifying identity currently worn by a soldier around his or her neck. During the Mine Run campaign in the fall of 1863, troops began writing out brief forms of identification and pinning these notes onto their clothing before entering battle.

In the fall of 1864, the 18th Army Corps, under General C. G. Ord, and General Birney's X Corps were ordered to block Confederates from resupplying Petersburg, Virginia. On September 27, two days before the Battle of New Market Heights, of which Chaffin's Farm was a part, acting adjutant general of the 4th U.S. Colored Regiment Samuel W. Vannuys wrote this note from his camp at Dutch Gap, Virginia.

★

Should I die upon the field of battle for the sake of a loving Mother and Sister, inform my Father—John H. Vannuys, Franklin, Indiana— of the fact.

Head Quarters 3d Brigade 3d Division 18th Army Corps,
Camp, at Dutch Gap Va.
, Sept 27, 1864.

This Testament belongs to Captain S. W. Van nuys. Acting Asst Adjt General 3ᵈ Brig. 3ᵈ Div. 18ᵗʰ A.C. Should I die upon the field of battle for the sake of a loving Mother and Sister inform my Father — John H. Van nuys, Franklin Indiana of the fact. Mr. John H. vanings it is my painful duty to inform you that your Son was Killed on the 29ᵗʰ

Courtesy of the Gilder Lehrman Institute of American History, New York

African Americans from Vannuys's 4th as well as soldiers of the 6th U.S. Colored Regiment fought a brief but fierce battle to capture Southern fortifications at Chaffin's Farm. Of the 1,300 African American soldiers, more than one-third were killed or wounded, the 4th suffering the most deaths during the battle. The heroism displayed by these poorly trained but proud troops was astonishing. More than 21 Medals of Honor were awarded to African Americans during the Civil War; approximately 13 were earned during this battle alone, which engaged nearly 30,000 men from both sides. Days after the fighting, as corpses were being removed from the field, Vannuys's body and ID were found by a Confederate soldier, known only as "L. B. F." He sent the paper dog tag back to John Vannuys in Indiana, adding this chilling note.

Mr. John H. Vanings it is my faithful duty to inform you that your son was killed on the 29th of the last month near chaffins farm, VA, I have his testament. I will send if you wish it from your enemy one of the worst rebels you ever seen.

PRIVATE ARNOLD RAHE TO HIS PARENTS,

U.S. Army Air Force, England, September 1943,

World War II

Just a few months after the attack on Pearl Harbor and America's entry into World War II, the first group of 1,800 U.S. Army Air Force personnel arrived in Liverpool, England. By the end of August 1942, in preparation for battle in the skies over Europe, they were operating nearly 400 aircraft, including B-17s, P-38s, and C-47s. Rahe's last flight might have been as a member of the operation against ball-bearing factories in Schweinfurt, Germany, on October 14, 1943. Remembered as the greatest air battle in Air Force history, it became known as "Black Thursday" because of the 60 B-17s shot down over enemy territory.

★

Dear Mother and Dad,

Strange thing about this letter; if I am alive a month from now you will not receive it, for its coming to you will mean that after my twenty-sixth birthday God has decided I've been on earth long enough and He wants me to come up and take the examination for permanent service

B-17 bomber in a mission over Germany

with Him. It's hard to write a letter like this; there are a million and one things I want to say; there are so many I ought to say if this is the last letter that I can ever write to you. I'm telling you that I love you two so very much; not one better than the other but absolutely equally. Some things a man can never thank his parents enough for; they come to be taken for granted through the years; care when you are a child, and countless favors as he grows up. I am recalling now all your prayers, your watchfulness—all the sacrifices that were made for me when sacrifice was a real thing and not just a word to be used in speeches. I know how you had to do without things to put me through school. You thought I didn't realize these things, but I did.

For any and all grief I caused you in this twenty-six years, I'm most heartily sorry. I know that I can never make up for those little hurts and

For any and all grief I caused you in this twenty-six years, I'm most heartily sorry.... It's a funny thing about this mission, but I don't think I'll come back alive....

real wounds, but maybe if God permits me to be with Him above, I can help out there. It's a funny thing about this mission, but I don't think I'll come back alive. Call it an Irishman's hunch or a pre-sentiment or whatever you will. I believe it is Our Lord and His Blessed Mother giving me a tip to be prepared. In the event I am killed you can have the consolation of knowing that it was in the "line of duty" to my country. I am saddened because I shall not be with you in your life's later years, but until we meet I want you to know that I die as I tried to live, the way you taught me. Life has turned out different from the way we planned it, and at twenty-six I die with many things to live for, but the loss of the few remaining years unlived together is as nothing compared to the eternity to which we go, and it will be well worth while if I give my life to help cure a sickened world, and if you and I can help to spare our mothers and fathers and younger generations from the griefs of war.

As I prepare for this last mission, I am a bit homesick. I have been at other times when I thought of you, when I lost a friend, when I wondered when and how this war would end. But, the whole world is homesick! I have never written like this before, even though I have been through the "valley of the shadows" many times, but this night, Mother and Dad, you are very close to me and I long so to talk to you. I think *of you and of home. America has asked much of our generation, but I am glad to give her all I have because she has given me so much.*

Goodnight, dear Mother and Dad. God love you.

Your loving son,

(Bud) Arnold Rahe

2ND LIEUTENANT SHIGEYUKI SUZUKI TO HIS PARENTS,

Kyushu, Japan,

1944–1945,

World War II

The historical deification of Japan's emperor, along with the country's burgeoning militarism in the twentieth century, profoundly influenced Japan's educational system. Many young men were instructed that martyrdom in service to the emperor and country was not only acceptable, but also honorable. However, by 1944, the strength of Japan's military had been substantially reduced. Harkening to the *kamikaze*, the "Divine Wind" typhoon that destroyed the Chinese invasion fleet of Kubia Kha in 1281, the Japanese High Command created the Kamikaze Special Attack Squad. Using bomb-laden planes, the kamikaze volunteers willingly flew one-way missions in the hope of smashing into enemy ships.

The first organized suicide aircraft raid was on October 25, 1944, when kamikaze pilots flew against the American aircraft carrier *St. Lo* during the Battle of Samar in the Pacific. Formerly known as the *Midway*, the ship was renamed to commemorate the American victory in St. Lo, France, and to make way for a larger carrier bearing the same name. A single Zero plane, still armed with its bombs, slammed into the flight deck and ignited the ship's own munitions. The *St. Lo* rolled over and sank in half an hour.

The following letter provides insight into a kamikaze's rationale.

People say that our feeling is of resignation, but that does not know at all how we feel, and think of us as a fish about to be cooked.

Young blood does flow in us.

There are persons we love, we think of, and many unforgettable memories. However, with those, we cannot win the war.

To let this beautiful Japan keep growing, to be released from the wicked hands of the Americans and British, and to build a "free Asia" was our goal from the Gakuto Shutsujin year before last; yet nothing has changed.

The great day that we can directly be in contact with the battle is our day of happiness and at the same time, the memorial of our death.

Between 1,220 and 4,000 Japanese volunteers gave their lives in a program that destroyed or sank 56 Allied ships and damaged hundreds more.

PRIVATE 1ST CLASS RICHARD E. MARKS TO HIS MOTHER,

Vietnam, December 12, 1965,

Vietnam War

Richard grew up in California and Eastchester, New York, and at 18, a year after his father's death, he enlisted in the United States Marine Corps. Arriving in Vietnam in May 1965, he was promoted to Private 1st Class, and served with Company C, 1st Battalion, 3rd Regiment of the 3rd Marine Division. He died on Valentine's Day 1966, at the age of 19, during combat at a forward outpost north of Da Nang. He has headed this letter, "Last Will & Testament of PFC Richard E. Marks."

Dear Mom,

I am writing this in the event that I am killed during my remaining tour of duty in Vietnam.

First of all I want to say that I am here as a result of my own desire—I was offered the chance to go to 2nd Marine Division when I was first assigned to the 4th Marines, but I turned it down. I am here because I have always wanted to be a Marine and because I always wanted to see combat.

I don't like being over here, but I am doing a job that must be done—I am fighting an inevitable enemy that must be fought—now or later.

I am fighting to protect and maintain what I believe in and what I want to live in—a democratic society. If I am killed while carrying out this mission, I want no one to cry or mourn for me. I want people to hold their heads high and be proud of me for the job I did.

There are some details I want taken care of. First of all, any money that you receive as a result of my death I want distributed in the following fashion.

If you are single, I want you and Sue to split it down the middle. But if you are married and your husband can support you, I want Sue and Lennie to get 75% of the money, and I want you to keep only 25% —I feel Sue and Lennie will need the money a lot more.

I also want to be buried in my Marine Corps uniform with all the decorations, medals, and badges I rate. I also want Rabbi Hirschberg to officiate, and I want to be buried in the same cemetery as Dad and Gramps, but I do not want to be buried in the plot next to Dad that I bought in mind of you.

That is about all, except I hope I never have to use this letter—

I love you, Mom, and Sue, and Nan, and I want you all to carry on and be very happy, and above all be proud—

Love & much more love,

Rick

The Marine Corps held Rick's letter until they presented it to his mother following his funeral at Arlington National Cemetery on February 21, 1966.

Final Thoughts

ELEANOR WIMBISH
TO HER SON WILLIAM R. STOCKS,

Glen Burnie, Maryland, February 13, 1984,

Vietnam War

Billy Stocks, a helicopter pilot who served in Vietnam in the 23rd Infantry Division, was killed in action in 1969. His mother, Eleanor Wimbish, leaves letters for him beneath his name etched in black stone on the Vietnam Veterans Memorial in Washington, D.C. Since writing the letter that appears below, Mrs. Wimbish has both served on Maryland's Korean War Memorial Commission and been played by actress-singer Maureen McGovern in a play entitled *Letters from 'Nam.* Her deeply moving epistolary memorial to her son is the finest I've ever read.

Dear Bill,

Today is February 13, 1984. I came to this black wall again to see and touch your name, and as I do I wonder if anyone ever stops to realize that next to your name, on this black wall, is your mother's heart. A heart broken 15 years ago today, when you lost your life in Vietnam.

And as I look at your name, William R. Stocks, I think of how many, many times I used to wonder how scared and homesick you must

Jim told me how you died, for he was there and saw the helicopter crash. He told me how you had flown your quota and had not been scheduled to fly that day.

have been in that strange country called Vietnam. And if and how it might have changed you, for you were the most happy-go-lucky kid in the world, hardly ever sad or unhappy. And until the day I die, I will see you as you laughed at me, even when I was very mad at you, and the next thing I knew, we were laughing together.

But on this past New Year's Day, I had my answer. I talked by phone to a friend of yours from Michigan, who spent your last Christmas and the last four months of your life with you. Jim told me how you died, for he was there and saw the helicopter crash. He told me how you had flown your quota and had not been scheduled to fly that day. How the regular pilot was unable to fly, and had been replaced by someone with less experience. How they did not know the exact cause of the crash. How it was either hit by enemy fire, or they hit a pole or something unknown. How the blades went through the chopper and hit you. How you lived about a half-hour, but were unconscious and there-fore did not suffer.

He said how your jobs were like sitting ducks. They would send you men out to draw the enemy into the open and then they would send in the big guns and planes to take over. Meantime, death came to so many of you.

He told me how, after a while over there, instead of a yellow streak, the men got a mean streak down their backs. Each day the streak got bigger and the men became meaner. Everyone but you, Bill. He said how you stayed the same, happy-go-lucky guy that you were when you arrived in Vietnam. How your warmth and friendliness drew the guys to you. How your [lieutenant] gave you the nickname of "Spanky," and soon your group, Jim included, were all known as "Spanky's gang." How when you died it made it so much harder on them for you were their moral support. And he said how you of all people should never have been the one to die.

Oh, God, how it hurts to write this. But I must face it and then put it to rest. I know that after Jim talked to me, he must have relived it all over again and suffered so. Before I hung up the phone I told Jim I loved him. Loved him for just being your close friend, and for sharing the last days of your life with you, and for being there with you when you died. How lucky you were to have him for a friend, and how lucky he was to have had you.

Later that same day I received a phone call from a mother in Montana. She had lost her daughter, her only child, a year ago. She needed someone to talk to for no one would let her talk about the tragedy. She said she had seen me on [television] on New Year's Eve, after the Christmas letter I wrote to you and left at this memorial had drawn newspaper and television attention. She said she had been thinking about me all day, and just had to talk to me. She talked to me of her pain, and seemingly needed me to help her with it. I cried with this heartbroken mother, and after I hung up the phone, I laid my head down and cried as hard for her. Here was a mother calling me for help with her pain over the loss of her child, a grown daughter. And as I sobbed I thought, how can I help her with her pain when I have never completely been able to cope with my own?

They tell me the letters I write to you and leave here at this memorial are waking others up to the fact that there is still much pain left, after all these years, from the Vietnam War.

But this I know. I would rather to have had you for 21 years, and all the pain that goes with losing you, than never to have had you at all.

Mom